COMPUTERS—

How to Break into the Field

By L. Peter Carron, Jr.

LIBERTY PUBLISHING COMPANY
Cockeysville, Maryland

Published by:
Liberty Publishing Company, Inc.
50 Scott Adam Road
Cockeysville, Maryland 21030

Library of Congress #82-082844
ISBN 0-89709-034-9

The publisher and the author thank the following people: Steve Miller for his editorial help; and Jay Little, MSGT, USAF, Computer Operations Supervisor, for his technical and editorial assistance.

Manufactured USA

To my wife, Jean, and
daughter, Lynn

A special thanks to my brother, Damon,
who provided immeasurable assistance
in the preparation of this book

I feel that one who is preparing for the job hunt would benefit by reading this handbook...I would recommend this text for those who wish to enter the data processing field.

Dr. Dana H. Verry, Phd., CDE, CBE
Executive Director, Emeritus
The Society of Data Educators

Contents

Introduction 1

Unlimited Career Opportunities 3

Don't Be Intimidated! 7

Job Choices 19

How to Get Started 39

Getting Your Data Processing Education 57

Computer Languages Explained 69

The Many Applications of Computers 93

Thorns Among the Roses 117

Key Information Sources 125

Glossary of Terms 146

Index 149

Acknowledgements 153

Introduction

Over the years, I've met a great many people who have expressed a strong desire to work in the field of data processing. The fact that computers is a rapidly-growing business with many opportunities is, of course, no secret. Perhaps this attraction stems from a fascination with computers or from an aspiration to become involved in a well-paying field with a good, secure future. It makes little difference. Experienced or not, anyone willing to learn and to work has a reasonable chance to break into this field.

Although their backgrounds may vary, the questions these people ask are similar: "Is it difficult to learn to program a computer?", "What is the best programming language to study?" and "Employers prefer experienced personel– so how can *I* get started?". This book will answer these and many other questions. It will explain the business in general, and it will explore the many job opportunities opening today and in the years ahead.

This book was written as a stepping stone for students, job seekers and career changers. There is no magic formula between these covers. However, if you use this book as a guide, set your goals, and make a sincere effort, the sky is the limit!

L. Peter Carron, Jr.
October, 1982

1

Unlimited Career Opportunities

The ever-widening application of computers to business, science, education — in fact to nearly all aspects of modern life — has generated intense interest and excitement. For many, the real excitement starts with the realization that data processing offers excellent job opportunities. Indeed, it is a challenging and well-paying field.

The prospective data processor may be lured by the prestige of the industry, or by the high pay computer professionals command. Or job security may be the lure, especially to those who have seen jobs come and go in uncertain economic times. Whatever the initial reason for considering the data processing field, almost everyone is now aware that the demand for qualified data processing personnel remains strong in both industry and government as the computerization of the work place goes on.

A bonus for many considering the computer field is that it is truly one of equal opportunity. Men and women are equally adept at data processing with women being found in positions at all levels. Furthermore, positions in the computer profession may be ideal for the handicapped, who will find that this field offers advancement possibilities to movement-restricted people, and even blind individuals.

Many positions do not require a great deal of education. If an individual updates his or her skills to keep pace with technological advancements, data processing can be a lifetime profession.

People from many different backgrounds are able to enter the field. Former accountants, teachers, clerks, retirees, economists, psychology majors, draftsmen, social workers, electronic technicians, cement workers and industrial engineers are among those who have become data processors.

For future job candidates, perhaps the most important consideration is the employment prospects of this profession.

According to the latest available U.S. Department of Labor statistics, there are more than 1½ million people currently employed in the computer industry in the following capacities:

Computer operating and data entry personnel - 700,000
Computer programmers - 260,000
Systems analysts - 200,000
Computer service technicians - 70,000
Computer manufacturing personnel - 270,000
Computer salespeople - 11,000

These current numbers show only part of the story, however. Projections of future statistics for the computer industry are even more impressive.

The U.S. Department of Labor statistics also show the computer industry to be one of the fastest growing in the country. Certain job opportunities within the industry are projected to outpace the supply of qualified personnel for years to come. By the year 1990, employment opportunities for programmers are projected to increase by more than 20 percent from current levels. A 25 percent increase is projected for systems analysts and an increase of at least 40 percent is projected for computer manufacturing jobs. However, these figures are from government sources.

Many private industry groups report on these same statistics and are more optimistic. In other words, on the

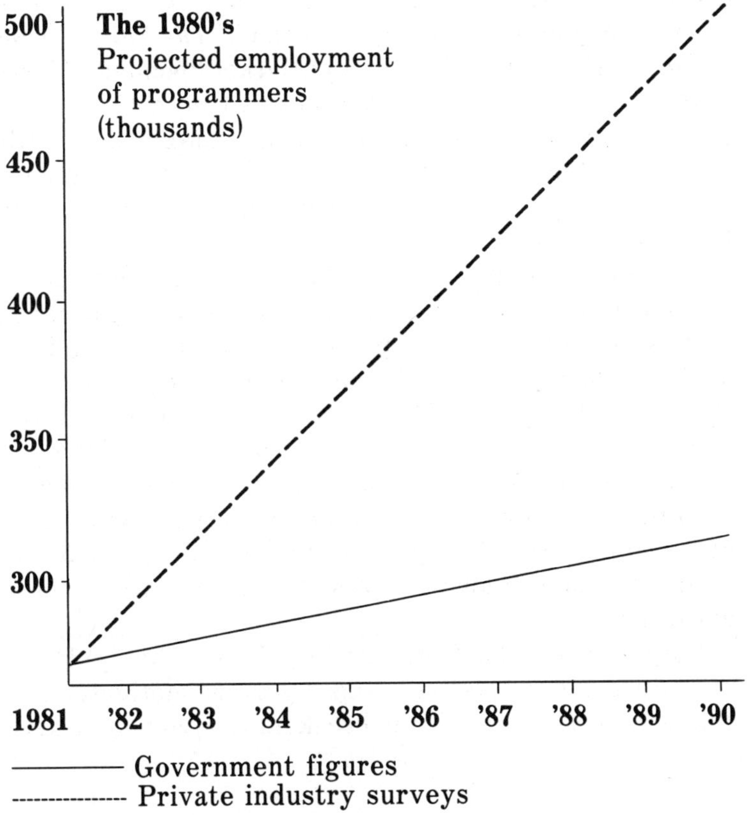

average, statistics from private industry sources show a much greater demand for data processing personnel in the coming years. For example, a national survey conducted by one of the well-known computer industry magazines found the increase in demand for programmers to be *four times greater* than that shown by government figures. Other industry surveys have shown comparably high statistics.

Regardless of the source of the figures, employment opportunities in data processing can only be described as bright. Newspaper headlines throughout the country attest to this fact. To quote just a few: the *New York Times* shows "Computer Personnel in Demand," *The Philadelphia Inquirer*" says, "What Recession? Market Booming in Computer Jobs," and *Computerworld* has run many articles such as "Computer Grads Top Most Wanted List," "DP Staffers Remain Tops in Demand," "Computer Graduate Seen as a Hot Item" and "Programmers Number 1 in Employer Demand."

There is no doubt about it. This is a good field to be in, and it looks like it will stay that way for a long time to come.

It is possible that you possess some of the qualities needed to become a good data processor. Are you a logical thinker? Can you type? Do you enjoy a challenge? Are you a creative thinker? Do you like to tackle puzzles? Are you well organized? Are you good at math? Do you like to deal with people? Do you have a keen interest in computers? Many jobs in the data processing field are filled by individuals who can answer "yes" to one or more of these questions.

Forget about what you currently do for a living. If you are interested in this area, and if you are motivated and willing to work hard, *you* can break into the computer field.

2

Don't Be Intimidated!

The use of computers is so widespread today that you've probably used one just recently without thinking about it. Automated or 24-hour teller systems at banks are computer controlled, for example. So are most telephone company switching systems, especially since the push button tone dial system came into use. Even if you haven't used a computer directly, the chances are someone is using a computer for you today. Credit card charges, payroll checks, book and record clubs, magazine subscriptions . . . these are but a few of the many uses of computers which have an influence on your life every single day.

In effect, nearly everyone is using or making use of a computer one way or another. Yet many people are still a little afraid of them. Perhaps the science fiction movies which show robots with the blinking lights and whirring sounds taking over the world, or machines that explode when the wrong information is entered are reasons people have become intimidated. Your bank's automated teller may confiscate your card if you press the wrong ID number too many times. But it won't explode. Good tools are not dangerous.

Computers *are* tools, and they are not especially mysterious. What the computer-tool does for us is relatively simple. It adds, subtracts, multiplies and divides faster than we can. It can compute ten, a hundred, maybe even a million times faster than we can. This multiplies our ability in much the same way a lever does: it allows each person to do more work with less effort.

There are several components to a computer which enable the machine to perform these feats of calculation. The components may all be in a single cabinet or may be arranged in several sections like a stereo system. In any case, all computer systems involve the same basics.

First there is what might be called the heart of the computer: the Central Processing Unit, or CPU. This is the section of the computer which deals with the electronic manipulation of data. In older computers it was an entire section of the cabinet. In today's newest microcomputers, the CPU can be found in a package smaller than a shoebox.

All the calculations in the world aren't any good without a memory. This is what is attached next to the CPU. In older computers, the memory directly attached to the CPU is known as *Core* memory because the information was stored on tiny bits of ferrite wrapped in a magnetic field. More common today is RAM, for Random Access Memory, and pronounced just like the animal. The amount of RAM is one of the measures of the power or ability of a computer because the information stored in RAM is immediately available to the CPU for calculations. RAM memory might be the old Core type material or it could be one of the newer forms of storage on disk, "floppy disk," or chip. Another type of memory, ROM (Read Only Memory), is used for long-term storage and takes longer to process.

Tape drives, for example, are used for ROM storage. Variable data information is normally stored, written or retrieved from the RAM. This is a temporary storage of data and when the power is turned off, all the stored data is lost. ROM, on the other hand, is used for the permanent retention of information such as program instructions, program tables and other types of fixed data. When the power is turned off to this unit, all the stored data is retained.

Attached to the CPU is a controller (or in a microchip system, a special switch circuit) which acts as a switchboard for the computer. The controller, or channel controller on larger systems, routes the incoming and outgoing information to the appropriate spots. Outgoing information goes to various peripherals for storage or display, while incoming information may be sent to the RAM or used to instruct the CPU.

The peripherals can be anything from a teletype machine, to a Cathode Ray Tube display unit (often simply referred to as a "CRT"), to a tape drive for information storage. In home computers or small business applications, the tape may be merely an updated version of a standard cassette tape you might play in your car stereo. Larger systems use reel-to-reel tapes and/or disks.

Oddly enough, many people think the various peripheral devices *are* the computers. TV shows and movies frequently show bank after bank of tape drives (which are merely memory storage) or CRT screens with their ominous messages when they want to show a computer facility. These are not the computers — they are peripherals; the so-called "bells and whistles."

A TYPICAL SMALL COMMERCIAL COMPUTER SYSTEM

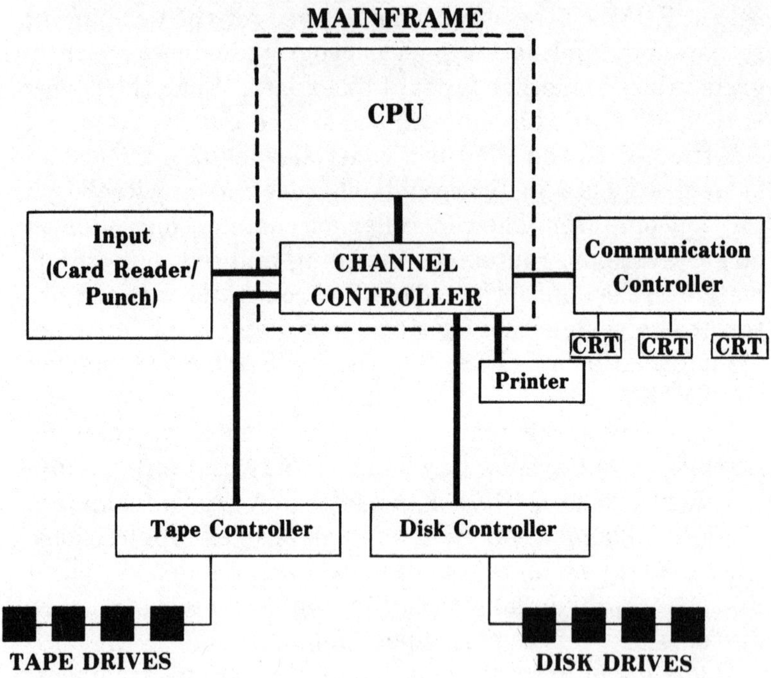

Computer Mainframe – Includes the CPU, channel controller(s), storage controller(s) and the master console.

CPU (Central Processing Unit) – Part of the computer mainframe. Through circuits, the CPU interprets and executes program instructions.

Channel Controller – Coordinates and controls the data traffic over the various channels (e.g., to and from the disk controller, or the tape controller, or the communication controller, or any other input/output device).

Disk Controller – Controls all disk drives assigned to that channel.

Disk Drive – A mechanism for rotating a disk pack (a series of magnetic disks designed to hold computer information) and controlling its movements.

Tape Controller – Controls all tape drives assigned to that channel.

Tape Drive – A mechanism for moving a magnetic tape (a tape that is wrapped on a reel and designed to store computer information) and controlling its movements.

Communication Controller – Controls all CRT units assigned to that channel.

CRT (Cathode Ray Tube) – An electronic vacuum tube, similar to a television picture tube, that is used to display graphic images. Although CRT terminals are now the most widely used method of display in offices, smaller, flat panel (plasma screen) displays are also becoming popular.

Printer – An output device that produces, on paper, a final copy of the data.

"This is my pride and joy. It set us back $127,000 and it costs us $900 a month for maintenance, but it's completely taken over Mrs. Crabswacker's Friday afternoon chore of preparing the payroll."

The IBM Personal Computer Today, the principles of data processing are being introduced to youngsters at earlier ages than ever before. The impact of computers on our society has only just begun.

The IBM Professional Office System Computers are no longer the exclusive tools of only large businesses and government agencies. Microcomputers and minicomputers are now being used by individuals and small businesses in almost every imaginable way.

A good place to see a business-sized computer system "in person" is at a business trade show. Most larger cities have five or ten such shows a year and even smaller cities have one or two. There you might see a dull gray or vinyl-white cabinet the size of a refrigerator or somewhat smaller, hooked into a keyboard or TV-type screen. That cabinet *is* the computer!

If you do get a chance to see computers at a trade show, you'll want to collect much of the information offered at the show. You'll find bookkeeping computers, word processing computers, and other special-application computers, as well as more generalized systems.

Also at the trade show, you will find references to the languages or language the computers use. Some systems offer a choice, while others come with only a single language. A computer language is not a spoken language, but rather it is a series of definitions and rules, written out, which make the computer work for you.

A later chapter deals with programming in more depth, but the basic concept behind programming is that tasks have to be broken down into their constituent parts. An analogy here might be helpful to illustrate this point.

Imagine that you are a carpenter and you've discovered you're out of ten penny nails. You simply say to your helper: "Go to the hardware store and buy five pounds of ten penny nails."

If you break that order down you might have to say "Go get my keys from my coat, take the red truck down to the Hiway Four Hardware Store, and pay cash for five pounds of ten penny nails."

For a slow learner or new helper you might have to give exact directions to the store, explain how to use the choke on the truck, etc. Well, a computer is just like that slow or new helper. It needs everything clearly spelled out to get the project done. Yet once the program is written successfully it can be used over and over, just the way a helper will learn how to get to the hardware store. The difference is that the computer *cannot* vary from your program. It does exactly what you tell it to do, and only that. Like a new helper, it might run out of gas because you forgot to tell it to check the gas in the truck.

Another place to see a computer up close is a computer store. These are relatively new and increasingly popular outlets in the marketplace. But today, you'll find them carrying small-business and home computers of all types. In some cases, you can go to a store, buy your computer, take it home with you, and be "up and running" the very same day!

Although most computer stores only carry the smaller computers, even these systems will give you a good understanding of what a computer is and what it can do. Also at computer stores will be material on various special applications and on programming languages. You'll find many brochures on the equipment the store carries. Many computer stores also offer beginning courses in programming for those interested in learning BASIC, PASCAL, and other computer languages. These courses are not the same as taking a course from a computer school, but they will give you an idea of what is involved in programming. If your local store also includes a "users group," you may find some excellent assistance in deciding which language you might want to learn.

Throughout this book, a high school education is suggested as the minimum for the field of data processing. This is really a standard established by employers in general. Currently, computer programming and related courses are being taught to youngsters in Junior High School. Therefore, if you have a high school diploma or a high school equivalency you should, at the very least, be able to learn the basic skills required by this industry.

Here are a few more words you may need to know before you continue with this book. Just read them over once or twice to get a feel for the jargon. You'll also find more key data processing terms later in the glossary.

ABBREVIATED DICTIONARY OF DATA PROCESSING TERMS

ACRONYM - A word formed from letters of other words. For example, the word FORTRAN is derived from the two words FORmula TRANslation.

ALGORITHM - A step-by-step process which is used to solve a particular programming problem. An algorithm is usually represented pictorially by a "flowchart."

BUG - An error in a computer program.

COMMAND - A word or phrase entered into a computer for the purpose of instructing the computer to perform some function. COMMAND is also used to refer to certain words in a computer program. For example, the command "DIV" might instruct a program to divide one number by another.

COMPILE - To convert a source program (a program which a programmer has written) into an object program (a program which the machine understands).

CRT - Cathode ray tube. An electron tube, similar to a TV screen, which is used to display information from a computer system.

DATA - Basic element of information in a computer system.

DISK - A circular, rotating magnetic data storage device.

FIELD - Elements of data in a computer storage device

which comprise an assigned area for some specific purpose. For example, a name may comprise a field in a computer tape record which occupies positions 1 to 20 in that particular record. The street address may occupy positions 21 to 40 etc.

FILE - A collection of related data records stored on some type of computer storage medium. For example, a file of names and addresses on a disk storage device.

INFORMATION PROCESSING - A term used to refer to the processing of any and all types of information. Data processing is a somewhat more restrictive term, being a type of information processing.

INPUT - Data which goes into a computer system.

MACHINE LANGUAGE - A programming language which a computer system understands without translation. All other languages must first be interpreted in order to transform them into machine language. Only when a language is translated into machine language is it actually understood by the computer.

OUTPUT - Data put out from a computer system.

PROCEDURAL LANGUAGE - A computer programming language which is written in a step-by-step fashion, something on the order of READ this, GOTO there, PRINT that, etc.

READ - To sense information. For example, a computer reads information that is stored on magnetic tape.

RECORD - A group of related fields on a computer storage device. Records can be stored in cards, on tape, on disk and on other computer storage devices.

SOFTWARE - Computer programs and procedures for the operation of a data processing system.

TAPE - A long, thin strip of material with a magnetizable surface onto which data can be stored by magnetic recording. The standard length is 2,400 feet.

TIME-SHARING - The simultaneous use of a computer system by more than one user.

WRITE - To transfer data to an information storage device or an output device. For example, a computer can write a name and address file onto tape, from a name and address file that it has read from cards.

3
Job Choices

The tight job market in recent years has placed a greater value on experience in all areas of employment—the computer field is no exception. Even though new opportunities are opening up more readily in this field than in most, as a general rule, the more training or experience one has to offer, the easier it is to enter. Therefore, it is especially helpful to understand the various job categories and what employers expect at each level. As you will see, the opportunities are, indeed, unlimited.

This chapter describes eight data processing job classifications: Data entry operator, Computer/peripheral equipment operator, Telecommunications Network operator, Programmer, Systems programmer, Systems analyst, Data processing manager, and other jobs in the field. The first seven categories, each covered in detail, represent about eighty percent of all available jobs. If desired, many of these classifications can be separated into finer categories. For example, the U.S. Department of

Labor has defined the following list of data processing job classifications in their Dictionary of Occupational Titles:

Auxiliary-equipment operator
Card punch operator
Card-tape converter operator
Computer operator
Computer-peripheral equipment operator
Computer-tape librarian
Computer terminal operator
Keypunch operator
Keypunch operator, numeric
Keypunch verifier
Manager, electronic data processing
Program coder
Programmer, detail
Programmer trainee
Programmer-analyst
Programmer, business
Programmer, chief, business
Programmer, engineering and scientific
Programmer, information systems
Programmer, process control
Supervisor, computer operations
Supervisor, data processing

Working with the seven classifications mentioned will considerably simplify matters and make for easier understanding. In addition, many of the job titles listed by the Department of Labor will be found only in the largest computer installations, and cannot be considered as being representative of job titles in a typical installation.

Some jobs may have overlapping titles. For example, an individual can hold a single job requiring that person to be a combination data entry operator/computer operator, or a programmer/analyst or even a computer operator/programmer trainee.

Salaries are given for each job category. Salaries for any one job title can vary widely depending upon the company, its geographic location, the employee's educational background and years of work experience. The figures given were arrived at by taking an average of figures from government sources and private industry surveys.

Finally, it should be emphasized that the field of data processing is divided into the two broad categories of business data processing and scientific data processing. Business data processing is concerned with the use of computers for business applications such as sales, payroll, personnel reporting, inventory control and all accounting functions which are a part of the business world. Scientific data processing is concerned with the use of computers for scientific and engineering purposes. This includes computer usage in engineering and the physical sciences such as chemistry, physics, geology, astronomy, etc. This book deals primarily with business data processing systems.

Data Entry Operator

The job classification of data entry operator is a modern version of the better known job title of keypunch operator. A keypunch operator enters data onto cards or tape by use of a special device known as a keypunch. The keypunch converts the data into a series of punched holes in the cards or tape.

The type of keypunch with which the majority of us are familiar is the card-style keypunch. In this machine cards are placed in a hopper to the left of the operator and are automatically fed one at a time into a position in front of the operator. The operator keys data into a typewriter-like keyboard as each card arrives at a position in front of him. The keypunch converts letters and numbers which the operator just entered, into a series of coded holes which are punched in the cards. As each card is completed, it moves into a second hopper at the right of the operator.

A data entry operator enters data into some type of data recording device for immediate or future use by a computer system. A keypunch is one such data recording device. There are also many other types of devices.

Almost all data recording devices use a typewriter-like keyboard for data entry. But once the data is entered, it is handled differently by different machines. Some data may be recorded as punched holes in cards or tape, as described above. Some data may be recorded magnetically onto magnetic data storage mediums such as computer tapes or disks. A computer tape is a long, thin strip that has a magnetizable surface on which data can be stored. A computer disk is a flat, rotating circular data storage device. Some data may be fed directly into the computer for immediate use, and other data may be displayed on a cathode ray tube (CRT), a device that looks like a T.V. screen.

The data entry operator enters data from a "source document."This document is usually a piece of paper on which information is recorded. Typical information may include an employee's department number and number of hours worked, or a customer number and the amount of payment received from that customer. It could even be a program that a computer programmer has written. Literally any information may be recorded on a source document for entry into a data entry device by the data entry operator.

A data verifier is another type of data entry job. A data verifier re-enters the identical data originally keyed by the data entry operator. The data verifier literally keys over the first operator's work and, by so doing, detects any mistakes made by the data entry operator. A data verifier is not used extensively throughout the business community, however.

A data entry operator should be at least a high school graduate and a good typist. He or she should possess good manual dexterity, be capable of close attention to detail and be able to work for long periods of time in the same working position. Typing accuracy is a must. Some companies may require the operator to produce a specified quantity of work with a limited error allowance.

A data entry operator may advance to data entry supervisor. This position requires supervision of a number of data entry operators. Data entry operators might also advance to computer or peripheral equipment operators. This position is covered in the next subchapter.

The data entry operator is the only data processing job classification in which the number of job opportunities may decline rather than advance over the next several years. This would be the result of newer and more automatic data collection methods.

Today, the average data entry operator earns about $12 - 15,000 per year, and the average data entry supervisor earns somewhat more.

Computer/Peripheral Equipment Operator

A computer operator runs the computer. He is responsible for controlling all operations of the computer and must keep accurate records of all jobs run on the computer, assuring that they are properly executed and run in the correct sequence.

A peripheral equipment operator runs the auxilliary equipment associated with the computer. (Peripheral equipment operators are basically computer operator trainees who start out on peripheral equipment and later progress to a more senior position). Peripheral equipment may be controlled by the computer or may be operated independently of the computer. Some examples of modern-day peripheral equipment include printers, CRT terminals and magnetic tape units. Printers are devices that produce printed output from the computer on some type of continuous paper form. CRT terminals are data terminals that are equipped with a typewriter-like keyboard which is used for entering information. The information thus keyed in, and other information, is displayed on a screen for viewing. Magnetic tape units are units that are used to record data on magnetic tape reels. They look somewhat like, and function similar to, a standard home tape recorder.

The two job categories of computer operator and peripheral equipment operator are only separated in the larger computer installations. In small or medium-sized data processing departments, a single individual, having the title computer operator, performs both functions. Therefore, for the purpose of discussion throughout this book, the title of computer operator shall be considered to mean computer operator and/or peripheral equipment operator.

These jobs often involve using older types of peripheral equipment which include card sorters and collators. Card sorters are used to sort the general purpose cards (also called "IBM Cards" by old-timers) into any desired sequence. For example, by using the card sorter, IBM cards, keypunched with the names and addresses of customers, can be sorted in alphabetic sequence by customer name or in numeric sequence by zip code.

A collator is a device which is used to combine, or collate, two separate stacks of cards. For example, a stack of cards containing year-to-date payroll information may be collated with another stack of cards containing current pay-period payroll information. This collation is performed to bring together the two types of cards for any single individual.

Card sorters and collators are examples of peripherals that are becoming obsolete due to technological advances in the computer field. However, some of these devices are still in use, although rarely, in some early computer installations.

A computer operator must be alert, observant and able to think independently. The operator usually follows a notebook of procedure, generally called a "specific operations manual" and/or a "run book." This book is referred to frequently and constantly updated. Yet, even with this guide, situations often arise requiring the computer operator to make important operating decisions independently. Above all, the computer operator must be thoroughly familiar with the operations of the equipment he or she is using.

Educational requirements for a computer operator include at least a high school education. In addition, most operators undergo specific training by the company for which they work. Sometimes classes are offered by the computer manufacturer which may take several days to several weeks to complete. Some high schools, junior and community colleges and private data processing schools provide courses that prepare the student to become computer operator trainees. These will be discussed in Chapter 5, GETTING YOUR DATA PROCESSING EDUCATION.

A computer operator may advance to the position of lead operator, operations supervisor or programmer. Today, the average computer operator earns more than $15,000 per year and the average lead, or head computer operator earns almost $20,000 per year.

Telecommunications Network Operator

Telecommunications, which involves sending data over telephone or telegraph lines, is one of the fastest growing segments of the computer field today. This position is not found at all computer sites. However, where it is, there will amost certainly be at least one "specialist," or an entire staff of these technicians. This person is responsible for maintaining the direct line of communication between the computer and any remote site with input or output devices (I/O devices).

In this segment of the computer field, you cannot simply say: "I am going to attach this CRT to the computer (perhaps miles away) by telephone line." Special equipment is required to make it work. A modem (modular/demodulator) is commonly used to connect the I/O device to the computer. There will be a modem at each end for the purpose of maintaining the strength and timing of the signal between the I/O devices and the computer.

Tele-processing systems vary from one application to another. Consequently, as the field of telecommunications grows, experienced or well-trained people will have an advantage as these jobs become available. It will be important to know the type of data being transferred, the type of equipment being used, how to correct equipment failure, and so on. While the telecommunications field will have entry positions open, it will be easier to break into this segment as an experienced computer operator or with a prior communications background.

A telecommunications network operator can enjoy a salary of $25,000 to $40,000 or more annually. However, computer operators looking to advance will find it somewhat easier to move into a managerial position by concentrating on programming rather than moving into a network operator slot.

Programmer

Programmers write computer programs. Computer programs are instructions to the computer that tell the computer what to do; when to add, when to subtract, when to print, etc.

There are many types of programmers. For clarity, these different types can be placed into the two categories of business programmers and scientific programmers. These classifications are the same two classifications into which the field of data processing is divided. Business programmers write programs for business applications and scientific programmers write programs for scientific and engineering applications.

We can, if we wish, further break each of these categories into the two subcategories of junior programmer and senior programmer. Senior programmers are more experienced and are able to write more complex programs.

The difference between a programmer and a *good* programmer lies in the ability to use the equipment and its software. A good programmer will keep programs as short as possible and easy to trouble-shoot, make certain that the language is used to its best advantage, and keep the documentation current and accurate.

In computer installations employing systems analysts, the programmer works from problem descriptions prepared by the systems analyst. These problem descriptions include a detailed list of steps the computer must follow to obtain the desired results. This list of steps is converted by the programmer into a series of coded instructions called a computer program. Many data processing installations do not employ systems analysts, however. In these cases, the computer programmer actually holds the dual title of programmer/analyst. He is not only responsible for writing the computer programs but is also responsible for the work normally done by the systems analyst.

The requirements for programmers vary widely from company to company. Some companies will not hire a programmer without a four-year college degree. Other companies pay relatively little attention to educational background, but rather insist on a certain number of years of programming experience. A high school diploma is a minimum education requirement. Any schooling beyond high school is a plus. Experience counts a great deal.

Requirements also depend upon the type of programming being done. Programming for business data processing applications requires some knowledge of business systems. Programming for scientific and engineering applications requires a strong background in mathematics. For companies requiring a four-year college degree for business systems programming, the degree is typically in computer science, accounting or business administration. The degree required for scientific programmers is typically in mathematics, engineering or physics. Programming may be learned on the job, in high school, in community and junior colleges, in four-year colleges and in private data processing schools.

Programmers have excellent chances for advancement. They may become senior programmers, systems analysts or data processing managers. Programmers' salaries vary widely from company to company and depend to a great extent on the number of years of programming experience. Entry level programmers without a four-year college degree may start as low as $10,000 to $15,000 per year. Experienced programmers, with or without four-year college degrees, can earn $25,000 per year or more.

To help further clarify the difference between junior and senior programmers, and to emphasize how important a knowledge of systems is to the programmer, we should look in on an early Monday morning scene at the Acme Tool

Manufacturing Company. When we do so, we see the data processing manager, Bill, and a junior programmer, Ed, later to be joined by senior programmer, John. Ed, the junior programmer, did very well in the RPG II course he just finished, and the company has high hopes for him. His knowledge of business systems is limited, however. Ed currently makes $13,000 per year. John is an old hand at RPG II and is experienced in all types of business systems. His salary is $26,000 per year.

Bill starts to speak . . . .

Bill - "Good morning, Ed. I have a program all laid out for you to work on. It involves the update of the general ledger with the cash receipts."

Ed - "What's the report that's printing out there?"

Bill - "That's the Cash Receipts Journal."

Ed - "What's that?"

Bill - "Well, it's simply a daily listing of all money received for the day."

Ed - "And when that report prints out I'm supposed to update the general ledger?"

Bill - "That's right."

Ed - "How do I do that?"

Bill - "By accessing the general ledger file, called GENLED, and adding the amount to the appropriate field in the general ledger file."

Ed - "What amount to what field?"

Bill - "Take the field called CASHRCT from the cash receipts record and update the appropriate account in the general ledger."

Ed - "Don't debits and credits come into play somewhere around here? When you debit an account with a credit balance you're supposed to subtract from the account balance, aren't you? Or, maybe it's add to the balance, I forget."

Bill - "Something like that, yes. But before we get into that, don't forget you have to pick up the customer name from the customer master file in order to show it on the report."

Ed - "Okay, the customer name is in the file called VENDOR, right?"

Bill - "NO, no. The file called VENDOR is for vendor names and addresses, not customer names and addresses. You pick up the customer name from the customer master file, called CUSTMSTR."

Ed - "Hmm, I thought the vendor and the customer were the same thing."

Bill - "Forget the whole thing, Ed. I'll find another program for you to work on. In the meantime, study this material and we can talk about it tomorrow.
Later that same day . . . .

Bill - "Hi, John. I have a complicated program I'd like you to handle. You have to update the inventory with the shipments for Jones Company."

John - "Oh, yes, I was expecting that one sooner or later. Updating that inventory is always a problem. The darn key to the inventory file is 25 positions long, and includes the model number, style, product code, size and inventory location. I know the Shipment Record going into the program doesn't have all those fields in it either. I'll have to pick up some of the fields by accessing other files first. Maybe I'll even go so far as to break up the update of the inventory into several different programs. It might take a little longer, but will simplify things considerably, and there will be less room for error that way."

Bill - "Okay, whatever you think best is fine with me. By the way, don't forget we also have the problem of calculating the difference between various dates."

John - "Yes, I remember, and I've been thinking about it. Instead of coding a table of dates into the program, I think it would be better to set up some kind of separate date file to use. And something else; due to the crazy way the Jones Company enters their orders, we don't know the size breakdown when the order is first entered. That's going to cause a problem. What do you think?"

Bill - "I really hadn't given it much thought. Let me know your ideas on it later. You seem to be more familiar with the problem than I am, so I'll go along with whatever you think is best."

Interesting, wasn't it? It's rather obvious why John is being paid twice as much as Ed. Moreover, it will probably be a year, or maybe two, before Ed becomes as proficient as John, depending upon the quality of his training, the type of work to be done, and his willingness to learn.

Finally, a word about scientific programming. Since most scientific programming positions require expertise in the field of mathematics, anyone considering this type of work should take as many math courses as possible. Your background should include courses up to and including college algebra and trigonometry, and calculus if possible. The stronger your background in math and engineering, the better your chances of obtaining such a position.

Systems Programmer

A systems programmer is in charge of the software system packages that make the computer work. These packages are available from the manufacturer of the system with minor modifications to match the needs of each customer. Normally, a basic package, called an "Operating System Release," is purchased with the equipment, modified and fine-tuned for that system by the vendor and the in-house systems programmers. Updates to the original package make this an on-going process for the systems programmer.

Additionally, a systems progammer will also be responsible for sub-system programs. These are small, more specific programs that directly affect the way a computer operates.

It is worth noting, however, that the value of the position of a system programmer can be limited to the popularity of the software and hardware for which he or she is experienced. Demand for system programmers can be very high — especially for those people experienced on large, widely-used mainframe computer systems. Generally speaking, a systems programmer's salary is about $10,000 per year *more* than a programmer within a similar organization.

Systems Analyst

A systems analyst studies and analyzes systems. Usually these systems involve the processing of data in some type of business system environment. After this study is complete, the analyst translates the requirements of the existing system into the capabilities of a computer system. He then prepares specifications for a programmer to follow so the programmer may write the necessary programs to make the computer system function as required.

The analyst begins his work by meeting with various individuals involved with a system as it is currently functioning. He determines the exact nature of all problems involved with the system and determines what output is required from the system. For example, a company may currently be using a hand system to prepare its customers' invoices. (An invoice is a bill sent to a customer to request payment for goods purchased). Although the hand system functions reasonably well during periods of normal business activity, it is incapable of handling the increased volume of work during peak business periods. Preparation of customers' invoices is delayed during these peak periods and errors result when the work is rushed.

The analyst defines the invoicing system as it currently operates and prepares charts and diagrams that describe the system work flow. Keeping in mind the problems existing in the current system, he designs a new computerized system to eliminate these problems and to provide the company with the required system output. This output will include computer prepared invoices and various management reports. The end result of the analyst's work will include new diagrams, known as flowcharts, which pictorially describe the computer system and aid the programmer in designing programs.

Some analysts become involved with every conceivable type of system. A business systems analyst may work with accounts receivable, accounts payable, inventory, general ledger, payroll or any other type of business system. A scientific or engineering systems analyst may work, for example, on a system that analyzes stresses on steel beams, or a system that is designed to send a man to the moon.

In case you are not familiar with business system terminology: An accounts receivable system is one which keeps track of money owed to a company by its customers;

an accounts payable system keeps a record of money a company owes to its creditors; and an inventory system keeps track of goods a company has on hand. A general ledger system deals with financial reporting, and a payroll system is concerned with payroll information.

A systems analyst must be able to think clearly and logically. He must be capable of assimilating large amounts of data from many different sources and analyzing this data with an eye toward producing a working computer system to meet the requirements of his company. Many systems that he deals with may become quite complex. As a result, he must possess above-average intelligence. Further, because an analyst meets many different individuals involved with the system being studied, he should have an agreeable, pleasant personality to deal efficiently and effectively with others.

To achieve the title of systems analyst, one must have years of experience in data processing. This job experience is necessary for the analyst to fully comprehend the system he is studying.

Educational requirements for systems analysts vary widely, similar in this respect to the educational requirements for programmers. Some companies will insist on a four-year college degree, while others place a greater importance on work experience. Those companies requiring college degrees might typically look for degrees in business administration and/or accounting for their business systems analysts. Degrees in mathematics or engineering are often required for systems analysts who study scientific and engineering systems. Some companies may require advanced degrees for work on very complex systems.

Systems analysts have excellent chances for advancement and many become data processing managers. Systems analysts presently earn, on the average, \$20,000 to \$40,000 per year.

Data Processing Manager

Data processing manager is the highest ranking job title in a computer installation. Individuals holding this title are responsible for the operation of the entire data processing department. The range of authority and responsibility in this position extends over the systems analysts, programmers, computer operators and data entry operators. In smaller-sized installations, all of these positions report directly to the data processing manager. In larger installations, the data processing manager has assistants. They might include a head systems analyst, a lead programmer, a computer operations manager and a data entry supervisor. Each supervisor is responsible for his or her staff.

The data processing manager is responsible for seeing that the department runs smoothly and efficiently. He must determine the relative importance of each job received by the department. He must then ensure a continous flow of work by assigning priorities to these jobs and see that each job is completed on time. He is also responsible for the proper selection of all computing machinery, or "hardware," used in the department. In addition, he must confer with upper management and the heads of other departments to be certain that all concerned work together to produce the quantity and quality of work required.

Data processing managers attain the position only after years of experience. This experience frequently includes years of work as a systems analyst and/or programmer. On rare occasions, and only in the largest of computer installations, the data processing manager may be selected because of general management capabilities rather than expertise in the data processing field.

Educational requirements for this position are similar to those for programmer and systems analyst. Here, again, much depends on the company involved. Some insist on a four-year college degree or advanced degree, while other companies look only at years of experience in the field.

The average data processing manager earns between $20,000 and $60,000 per year. This wide salary range occurs because the title of data processing manager is given both to one in charge of a staff of 1,000 in one company, as well as one over a staff of two in another.

Other Jobs in the Field

This book deals primarily with the seven job classifications discussed in the preceding subchapters, but there are other types of jobs available as well. Such positions include maintenance and security, sales, education and manufacturing.

In recent years, the electrical and mechanical reliability of computers and related data processing equipment has improved markedly. The preventive maintenance schedule on the first all-electronic computer included replacing every one of 18,000 vacuum tubes each year. This meant that a team of repairmen had to replace an average of 70 vacuum tubes per day, in addition to performing any other repairs required on that machine.

Today, the story is much different. Modern electronic and mechanical technology has reduced the required maintenance on computers and related equipment to an amazingly low level. Despite this fact, computers do need repairs from time to time. This service is provided by the computer repairman, or customer service engineer, as he is sometimes called.

Computer repairmen install new computers and service existing computer equipment. Most of today's computer machinery is complex. As a result, the computer repairman must frequently attend schools to keep informed about the mechanical and electrical functionings of the equipment he maintains. Some repairmen may specialize in the repair of a particular model or line of computers. Others may work on a large variety of equipment. Most repairmen work 40 hours per week and do so during normal business hours. However, there will be times when they must work overtime and at times other than the regular daytime shift. Most repairmen are employed by computer manufacturers. A few are employed by computer users. Those who are employed by manufacturers may be required to travel widely as they are dispatched from one customer to another.

Salesmen who work in the computer field may sell computers, peripheral equipment or data processing supplies such as paper, forms, printer ribbons, computer tape reels, etc.

Those who sell computers or peripheral equipment usually work for the manufacturer of the line of equipment they are selling. Those who sell data processing supplies usually work independently.

Computer salesmen and peripheral equipment salesmen can enjoy a substantial income. This is especially true of those employed by larger and better-known equipment manufacturers. Such positions, however, usually require a four-year college degree and the personality traits expected of a successful salesman. These include the ability to communicate well, to present a good appearance and to demonstrate self-confidence and ambition. These positions also require an in-depth knowledge of the equipment being sold.

Those who sell data processing supplies enjoy varying degrees of financial success. Much depends upon the salesman's business contacts and the size of the companies to which he sells. A typical, smaller data processing supply company may employ several salesmen. These salesmen, and sometimes the owner of the company, usually spend the majority of their day on the road visiting various computer installations.

Data processing educators are needed in colleges, public schools, private schools and companies. Colleges and public schools usually require instructors to possess a four-year college degree or advanced degree. Private data processing schools are less likely to have stringent educational requirements for their instructors. Instead, they often accept instructors having years of job experience. Private companies often use experienced staff members to instruct newer company employees in various areas of data processing.

There are also occupations associated with the manufacture of data processing equipment and supplies. This category of occupations accounts for approximately 18 percent of all data processing related jobs. It includes the entire gamut of manufacturing job classifications from the engineer to the chemist, mathematician, physicist, statistician, programmer, draftsman, maintenance mechanic, production supervisor, assembly-line worker and clerk. This category of jobs is so diverse that is is impossible to cover it in any detail. It is mentioned here only to illustrate the variety of opportunities open in this ever-expanding field.

4

How to Get Started

This book discusses a broad spectrum of computer applications to illustrate the diversity of data processing careers. Yet it is unrealistic to cover every facet in depth in an introductory book. Instead, emphasis has been placed on those areas offering the most jobs for the most people: the business segments of the industry.

The majority of all computer-related jobs *are* in business processing systems, and businesses are much more likely to hire the new or inexperienced data processor. The educational requirements in business tend to be less restrictive than those in the sciences. Additionally, as businesses become more and more familiar and comfortable with the use of computers, as time passes, they will expand the applications of the equipment. Thus, your chances for advancement are higher in a business environment.

Secondly, emphasis here has been on the small to medium-sized company. Usually it is easier to get started with the smaller company because smaller companies have less stringent employment requirements. Moreover, they are likely to have lower educational demands than a large company might for equivalent job positions.

This is not to say that you will be able to sneak into the field without any education. Indeed, an entire section deals with obtaining your education. Experience shows, however, that many will be trying to break into the field from other lines of work, or with educational backgrounds from different fields, or with just a high school education. The purpose of this book is to help those who need the most help. Those who hold a master's degree in computer science already know how they will break into the computer field. They will do so on the strength of their educational background. But the man or woman who does not hold such a degree will have a more difficult time getting started, and should carefully read and apply the material discussed in later chapters.

It is possible to break into the field without a great deal of education, or with education and/or work experience from another field, because the skills required can be learned and there is such a shortage of qualified personnel in data processing that many employers are willing to forego their normally stricter employment requirements to obtain the necessary qualified employees. This is particularly true in the case of computer programmers.

Answers to Three Frequently Asked Questions

Your first job in the computer field, with or without an education in the field, will be the most difficult to get. Most employers want experienced personnel. The inevitable response to this is "How can I get experience if no one will hire me?"

First we should look at the reason why most employers insist on experienced personnel. There is a good reason for it. Take computer programming, for example. It takes a long time to become a proficient programmer and even a longer time to become a proficient programmer who is experienced on a specific computer system.

Question: Why does it take so long to become a good programmer?

Answer: Some programs are very complex. To program often takes every ounce of skill a programmer has acquired through years in the field. In cases such as this, the basics of programming are not sufficient. Instead, techniques of programming become important. To write such a program requires skill in programming techniques that can only be developed through years of programming experience.

Question: Why should it take so long to learn how to use a specific computer system, when you are already experienced in a particular programming language?

Answer: All computers are different. Just because a programmer has ten years experience writing in COBOL (a popular programming language) on an IBM computer system, does not mean that he can switch jobs at any time and be just as efficient programming for a Burroughs' computer system which also uses COBOL. The programmer must first learn the commands needed to make the Burroughs' computer perform as required. He must learn how the job control statements work. (Job control statements are commands that tell the computer which programs are to be run, and in what order.) There is much more that the programmer must learn about the new system on which he is working. Suffice it to say, there can be large differences between computer systems. And, as a result, employers prefer to hire someone who not only knows the programming language, but also the operations of their particular make and model of computer.

Question: Why do most employers want experienced personnel?

Answer: The answers to the preceding questions should have answered this question for you. However, for emphasis, we'll look at a hypothetical case-in-point:

An employer gives the same programming assignment to three programmers. The first programmer, a man with eight years experience writing in COBOL, finishes the program in 16 working hours. The second man, a programmer with six months experience, finishes the program in 54 working hours. The third man, a programmer trainee, never gets the program to work at all. This is a hypothetical case, but a very real possibility!

This entire discussion has been on programmers, but the same principle of experience applies in the other job classifications.

A data entry operator, for example, must know two things: how to type, and how to operate the data entry device with which he is working. Good typing skills are a must because the alphabetic portion of any data entry keyboard is identical to a standard typewriter keyboard. Few companies are willing to teach a data entry operator typing (see last chapter). If an individual is already a good typist, all that remains to be learned is how to operate a particular data entry device. Companies can vary on their requirements. Some insist that a data entry operator be familiar with a particular machine before he or she is hired. Others are willing to train a good typist on their data entry equipment because learning to use a specific piece of data entry equipment is not especially difficult. The task is minor compared to the task of training someone to type.

For computer operating positions, an employer will hire someone from outside the company, or will train someone from within the company. If an employer hires from the outside, he will usually insist that the individual have experience operating a computer identical or very similar to his own.

A systems analyst, being a notch above a programmer in job status, requires more experience and/or education than a programming position. A systems analyst is expected to be familiar with most of the common business systems and have the capacity to understand an employer's specific needs within these systems, or an employer's needs for some new system that may apply to that particular business.

The title of data processing manager refers to a position which demands managerial experience and an understanding of all phases of the data processing operation. Obviously, experience in the field weighs heavily when applying for such a position.

Breaking Into the Field With Minimal Education

Most individuals without education or experience in the field obtain their first job in one of the four ways listed below:

1. By switching careers within the same company, from a job not in the field of data processing to one that is.
2. Through personal contacts, or word of mouth.
3. Through advertisements placed by employers.
4. Through advertisements placed by employment agencies.

Method number one is preferable. This method pertains to current employees of a company who have the opportunity to begin in the field due to recent developments or changes within the company. For example, sometimes a data processing department needs additional help. Rather than advertising for help from outside the company, the department may search within the company for an employee willing to switch departments and become a data processing trainee. Talk to your supervisor and the personnel department for leads or suggestions. Furthermore, it is not unusual for the data processing department to be active during odd hours of the day (and sometimes late into the night). This is just one more thing in your favor if you go this route.

Other opportunities can occur in companies where the computer installation is designed and programmed by a consulting firm. After the firm finishes its job, an employee within the company may be put in charge of running the installation. Often this individual becomes a programmer trainee capable of solving any minor programming problems that arise after the consulting firm has gone.

Method two is a common way for those experienced in the field to obtain jobs; but it is more difficult for the inexperienced individual to follow this route. The newcomer usually has few contacts within the field. Nevertheless, call on friends, acquaintances, and any business associates who might be able to help. If you think about it, the number of friends-of-friends can sometimes be substantial.

You will have to work hard to use method three. Your best bet is to go after a position in which the employer is advertising for some type of "trainee," whether it be a data entry trainee, computer operator trainee, programmer trainee or just plain data processing trainee. When you see the word trainee, you know the employer is looking for a novice. You won't have to compete with those who are experienced in the field, and breaking in will be easier.

Method four is similar to method three, but is less appealing for several reasons. First, employment agencies charge fees for finding jobs. These fees are high. Many companies will pay an employment agency's fee if the agency fills the slot with an experienced, hard-to-find employee.

Most companies are less willing to pay the fee for a trainee-type position. Also, an agency will not work as hard to find a job for a trainee as it will for an experienced data processor. The agency realizes it can place the experienced person more easily, and for a higher fee.

There are agencies which specialize in data processing jobs. Almost all of these agencies are looking for experienced data processors or individuals with a computer science education. The fact that they are EDP (electronic data processing) specialists isn't much help to the individual with no education or experience in the field.

Regardless of which of the four methods you use, you really must start with no less than a high school education. Find a job with a company, preferably as some type of data processing trainee (the pay won't be very much) in their data processing department, or in a capacity as closely related as possible. Sometimes certain positions in the accounting department will meet this criterion. Obviously, the closer that starting job meets your objectives, the better off you will be.

Breaking into the field this way is the toughest way to go, but it definitely can be done. Many of the men and women in the field today did it in this manner. Observations show that a large portion of programmers, systems analysts and data processing managers in the medium to small-sized companies (not Bethlehem Steel or General Motors) started without a college degree, and still do not have a college degree. If any do have degrees, they probably did not major in computer science. Computer science is a fairly recent degree program. To clarify a point concerning educational requirements, you will notice reference to "medium to small-sized company." Programmers, systems analysts and data processing managers in most large companies will be required to have degrees, probably even graduate level degrees.

If you are able to obtain a college degree in computer science you will obviously be in a much better position. But if college is not in your future, you can still achieve your objectives if you are willing to work hard. Data processing is one of the few fields left where it is possible to make it big without a degree.

When you apply for a job as a trainee, the rules of assertiveness that apply in every other endeavor can be your key to success:

- Express your desire to get into the data processing field.
- Express your desire to learn.
- Express your willingness to continue your education on your own, or through company training.

Once you have found an opening in a company, coming as close to your data processing objectives as possible, your real work begins. Now you have to demonstrate to management that you will be the worker you indicated when you were hired. To do this, start studying!

For specific suggestions on what to study, see the Self-Study section of Chapter 5. If you plan to get into programming, be sure to study the language that is used on your computer system at work. Don't make the mistake of studying the wrong programming language. Also, many companies will send their employees to classes given by the manufacturer of their system. This is a common way that many employees have received their programming education. Manufacturers' courses are discussed in the Company Training section of Chapter 5.

If your employer is not willing to send you to school, you have other alternatives. If you do not have a junior, community or regular four-year college nearby, or if your local college does not provide the courses you feel are needed, you can educate yourself by home study. Many computer manufacturers are able to supply home study manuals without cost or for a nominal fee. Ask any computer salesman about this.

Join your local "user's group." A user's group is an organization which is comprised of employees of companies that use a particular manufacturer's computer, or employees of companies that use a certain type of computer system. The "Small Systems User's Group" is an example of a local organization of users of small computers. The group exists for the purpose of providing a forum for the exchange of ideas between computer system users. Organizations of this type frequently have guest speakers and members who speak on topics of interest. The newcomer can especially benefit from such an organization.

Join your local chapter of the Data Processing Managers Association (DPMA). The DPMA is a large, nationwide organization with many local chapters. You do not have to hold the title of data processing manager to join. This organization can provide you with valuable assistance and valuable personal contacts as well. Most computer salesmen can give you information on how to contact the DPMA or any other organization.

If you cannot attend local monthly meetings, you can always join a helpful organization by mail. Examples of these include the Association of Computer Programmers and Analysts and the Association of Computer Users. Associations like these provide magazines, bulletins, reports and directories; hold seminars and workshops, and some have phone-in reference services. Refer to the back of this book for a list of organizations and associations.

Subscribe to a periodical. A great deal can be learned from a good magazine. *Computerworld* is one example of a very popular magazine with data processing professionals. Again, see the back for a list of periodicals. In addition, many companies are willing to pay the cost of these magazines and the dues for any associations you may join. Ask your supervisor.

Buy some type of computer dictionary. Howard W. Sams publishes an excellent book called the *Computer Dictionary and Handbook.* Such dictionaries are not cheap, but are well worth their price. Data processing uses a language all its own. There is nothing more frustrating than listening to someone converse fluently in data processing jargon, while you sit there with a blank look on your face.

You must work hard to get ahead in this profession, just as in any other. And you will have to work harder than the individual with a special education or a degree.

Breaking Into the Field With Education and/or Experience in Another Field

The fields and/or educational backgrounds that are most conducive to entering the field of business data processing are, in approximate order of importance: Mathematics, Business, and Accounting. One of the most important requirements of being a good programmer is to possess a logical mind, capable of systematically approaching and solving a programming problem. Most people skilled in mathematics meet this criterion. Therefore, math is considered the area closest to computer science itself. Where do business and accounting come in? It is also an advantage to have the ability to understand the needs and business systems problems of the company for which you work. Only when a company's problems are first analyzed, can they be solved, with or without a computer. Obviously, a background in business and/or accounting would be helpful.

If you possess any of these qualifications you are ahead

of the game. If not, you're going to have a more difficult time getting started. Regardless, your method of starting will be almost identical to that just described in "Breaking Into the Field With Minimal Education." The only difference is that you stand a better chance of starting higher on the data processing job scale. Or you stand a better chance of starting with a larger company. If you have a four-year college degree, your best chance of starting in the field lies with the larger company since they will be more willing to spend the time and money to train a well-educated newcomer.

Obtaining your first job is almost a matter of salesmanship. Since you are not an experienced data processor, you will have to sell yourself to your prospective employer by expressing your ambitions to get into the field and your willingness to learn the ropes once you have started. If you have not read "Breaking Into the Field With Minimal Education" because you thought it did not apply to you, go back and read it. Much of that section will probably be of interest.

If you have been in your current line of work for quite a few years you may have to take a temporary salary cut to break into the computer field. Just how temporary this cut is depends upon many factors and your personal circumstances.

There are some unusual ways that an individual with education and/or experience in another field can break into data processing. These methods are covered in detail in Chapter 5, under the subheading entitled "Some Unusual Ways to Obtain Your Education and Break into the Field."

Breaking Into the Field With a Computer Science Education

Obtaining an education in the field of computer science cannot guarantee you a job there, but it will make your chances of finding one much better. Obviously, the more education you can get, the better your chances will be. A four-year college degree is preferable to a degree from a junior college, which is preferable to a degree from a private data processing school. If you already have this degree, no one need tell you how to get it. If you don't have this degree, the next chapter, GETTING YOUR DATA PROCESSING EDUCATION, will help you.

Those who have a computer science education will probably obtain the initial job in one of four ways:

1. A student about to graduate, may obtain a position through interviews which are held by prospective employers who visit the school.
2. Through personal contacts, or word of mouth.
3. Through advertisements placed by employers.
4. Through advertisements placed by employment agencies.

Method one is the preferable way to obtain a first-time job. It will save a lot of time and frustrtion if you are able to obtain a position, or at least complete your initial job interviews, while you are still in school.

The other three methods of starting are discussed in the section entitled "Breaking Into the Field With Minimal Education." Read that section if you have not already done so.

Differences Between Large and Small Companies

Some companies are larger than others. Some are *very* small, and others *very* big. Why devote an entire section to this fact of life? Because the differences between large and small are very significant in the data processing profession. These differences can affect your entire career, so you'll want to think about your goals and desires and compare them with the aspects of the large and small company that you see most satisfying. Each potential data processor will have to make a decision based on the kind of environment desired.

The following points are generalizations. They do not hold true in all cases, but are designed to allow you to make some basic assumptions about this field.

Positive points in favor of larger companies include the higher pay scale and better job security. Usually fringe benefits are better with the larger companies because they have more employees, are better established, and can afford better benefit programs. The big winners in any company's programs are those at the higher levels; whereas in entry level positions, the difference between pay scale and benefits between large and small organizations is less significant.

Also perhaps more favorable to the large-company employee are the training programs and staff-growth policies. In general, the larger company is much more likely to aid an employee's education (once employed) and to favor expansion of employee's skills through internal and external classes. At entry-level, or trainee level, larger organizations are also more likely to have real experts in their fields, which can improve the quality of the on-the-job training you will receive.

If large companies have the distinct advantage of having large staffs, and hence needing lots of employees, they have a corresponding disadvantage: it may be difficult for an employee who lacks the educational background of other employees to advance. Worse, lacking a degree but showing real ability may be a ticket to a dead-end, middle management position in the most lackluster backwater the company can find. This isn't because you ask for the position, but because the educational requirements for higher level positions are much stricter than for the lower level positions.

The advantage of transferring within the company you work for also goes to the larger organization. This may turn into a disadvantage of being asked to relocate or lose your position entirely. Of course, you can help to minimize this kind of problem by asking about such transfer policies when you join the company, or during the job interviews. If staying where you live now is important to you, be sure to add it to your thoughts when deciding to join a company.

Smaller companies have a number of advantages for prospective data processors. Although smaller companies may not pay as well at the top levels, they will likely be competitive with large companies at the entry level spots. Also, they will be more willing, in general, to accept you without a top-flight educational background.

Smaller companies may give you more responsibility more quickly than large companies. If that's for you, remember that small companies may lack the technical assistance available from large ones. If you run into a major problem with a program in a small company there may be no one to turn to for immediate help.

Another generality to consider: large companies tend to have large computers and small companies to have small computers. This is true of the main computer installation a company uses. Of course, many large companies now run mini and even microcomputers at branch offices. However, the size of the computer may well affect which language you'll use, and what version of the language you'll use.

Specifically, the majority of the large computers as well as many of the minicomputers use either COBOL or FORTRAN. Also popular is a language called PL/1. The newer languages tend to run on the smaller minicomputers and even the business-oriented microcomputers. If you decide that you like to work the new languages better, then you're probably going to be more interested in a smaller shop, where BASIC, or RPG II, or PASCAL, or the newer generation languages will be more frequently used.

BASIC is frequently taught in community college courses; it is also taught at many computer stores because BASIC tends to be the language of preference for today's microcomputers. This means someone entering a job with a small company can more easily come into the company with some experience in the language, which certainly could be a plus.

Computer languages are discussed in much greater detail in Chapter 6.

There are large companies . . .

One of the largest data processing installations -- McDonnell Douglas Automation Company

. . . and then there are
small companies . . .

A computer service bureau in northeastern Pennsylvania -- Computer Resources, Inc.

In a small company you may find yourself in charge of *all* of the company's needs in your area. You could be *the* programmer, *the* data entry operator, or *the* computer operator. This would give you a broad-based series of job experiences for moving upward or onward later on. In a comparable position at a large company you might find yourself working on accounts receivable for seven years without a break.

Along with the added responsibility you might have at a smaller company goes the advantage of being closer to the decision making process in general. Being in the data processing department of a small company will mean you'll be more likely to be involved in the process of change as it occurs, rather than being the victim of it, as often happens at larger operations.

If salary is going to be your prime consideration, then in most cases you'll want to opt for a larger company. For example, the data processing manager in a small company might be making $25,000 a year while the data processing manager in a large company can make $45,000 a year with the same title. Why the difference? Because in the large operation the data processing manager will be overseeing more people, more equipment, a larger budget and will be doing more in a general managerial vein than someone in a small company.

One point to remember when trying to pick your environment is that the top programming and system analyst consultants usually got a start in large companies (at the time they were the only companies which could afford computers) but as soon as possible moved into smaller companies or become independent freelancers. Here, of course, we're talking about the cream of the crop at the top of the field, and it isn't an option available to data entry operators or computer operators. The job satisfaction, rather than salary considerations, seems to be most important to these top people. Remember, too, that the top people in the industry tend to think of their first five to ten years in the field as a time of training. It takes time and practice to be the best. You can get there if you work at it.

5 Getting Your Data Processing Education

The amount of education you need depends on your aspirations within the field. Generally speaking, higher job levels require more education and lower job levels, less. This chapter has been divided into five different ways to acquire your education. Any of these methods may, of course, be combined with any other. You can, for example, attend college at night and receive company training during the day. Or you may go to a private data processing school and at the same time study some additional subjects on your own at home.

Self-Study

Self-study is any studying which you do on your own. This may consist of studying at home or taking courses at a local community college, or elsewhere.

If you want to study individual books on your own, the difficulty in selecting them will be compounded by not knowing what you want to do within the field. If you want to be a programmer you will find a large selection of good books available. If you want to do anything else, your choice of books will be narrowed considerably.

There are many good books written about programming. Most of these are devoted to a single programming language such as COBOL or FORTRAN or BASIC or some other language. For other job categories in the data processing field you must search hard to find a book even partially devoted to the line of work in which you are interested. There are not many books devoted to how to be a data entry operator, or how to be a computer operator or how to be a systems analyst.

Jobs such as data entry operator and computer operator, for example, are really jobs that relate to a specific piece of hardware. That is, a data entry operator must know how to operate a certain data entry device, and a computer operator must know how to operate a specific computer system. It is difficult to get this kind of knowledge from a generalized book on the subject. Most data entry and computer operator jobs are learned either through hands-on experience, or by studying manufacturer's manuals for specific pieces of hardware.

All computer manufacturers provide operating and programming manuals for their equipment. Some provide additional self-study courses in everything from data entry to computer operations or programming. If you currently work for a company that has a computer, ask the computer salesman what educational material his company is able to supply. This material is normally provided free of charge or for a nominal fee. In many cases, the company you work for will be willing to pay any fees incurred. Study all of the manufacturer's material you can. It is important to your success in the field that you know as much as possible about the operations of the equipment you are using.

Local community and junior colleges provide some of the best educational bargains available. Some community colleges hold evening courses on almost every conceivable subject, many of them in the field of computer science. If you are fortunate enough to be able to take advantage of such instruction, it will greatly enhance both your confidence and your job search effectiveness.

The first course to study, regardless of your aspirations in the field, is some type of introductory data processing course, such as "Basic Computer Concepts," "An Introduction to Computer Science" or "Fundamentals of Data Processing." If you wish to get into programming, perhaps your local college provides several programming courses such as Programming in RPG II, Programming in COBOL or FORTRAN Language Programming. For programmers a course in business systems is most valuable. Perhaps you can find a course such as "Business Data Processing Systems," "Data Processing Systems and Procedures" or "Systems Design and Development."

And finally, your self-study program should include the purchase of a computer dictionary, as suggested earlier. You will be able to use this dictionary throughout your career as a valuable reference manual. Refer to the "Information Sources" section of this book.

Company Training

Company training is broken down into three areas. Employees may conduct classes for other employees within the same company, employees may receive hands-on experience through on-the-job training and employers may send their employees to schools outside the company.

It is usually the larger companies which provide such things as employee-conducted classes for other employees. These classes may cover almost any subject, from data entry to management. You are fortunate if you are able to participate in such a program.

Many companies are also providing employees with self-teaching courses using video cassettes and/or in-house equipment. This, too, is an inexpensive and worthwhile method of obtaining an education, updating your talents, or expanding your knowledge.

A more common type of company-provided training is on-the-job training. On-the-job training can be the most valuable training of all. It consists of watching others perform the job you are to do, and it consists of doing that job yourself, under the supervision of a more experienced individual. On-the-job training can be applied to almost any job category, from data entry operator to computer operator, programmer or systems analyst.

Many companies are willing to send their employees to schools outside the company. Of course, some companies have what is known as a "tuition refund program" where they reimburse an employee for his tuition while attending college. Other employers send their employees to classes given by a computer manufacturer. These classes vary in length from one day to several weeks. Most are held during the regular business hours. You may be able to commute daily to these classes, or you may have to travel to a city where they are held and stay in a hotel for their duration. Classes may be held on lower level subjects such as computer concepts or include subjects such as advanced programming techniques and computer installation management. These classes can be quite valuable and you should take as many as the company is willing to support. Companies vary widely in what training they are willing to provide for their employees. Such courses cost the company money and employee time. Some employers are willing to pay whatever it takes, others are not.

Private Data Processing Schools

Private computer education schools vary in curriculum length from three months to two years. The average school provides about 530 hours of instruction. Private schools perform an important function in the area of data processing education, and some are excellent schools. However, they have been the brunt of some unfavorable publicity in recent years because some do a poor job of adequately training their students. The prospective student is advised to carefully check the school and its reputation.

The most important items to question when judging a private computer school are:

1. What are the instructors' qualifications?
2. Does the school use modern data processing equipment?
3. Does the school teach modern data processing techniques and modern programming languages?
4. What percent of the students obtain employment in the field upon graduation?

If you are able to obtain favorable answers to these questions, a private school may be the answer. Private schools represent one of the fastest ways to break into the field without a computer science education. The individual who attends a good school and can maintain an above average class standing may find he is able to get a good start in the field upon graduation.

There are also private schools that teach only data entry techniques. These classes can range from three to fourteen weeks in length. Make sure the school in question uses modern data entry devices. Some still use the old style card keypunches, now becoming obsolete.

Community, Junior and Four-Year Colleges

Many prospective entrants into the field are attending community and junior colleges for their education. Some of these schools provide an education at a very reasonable price. Programs typically last about two and one-half years and lead to an associate degree.

Credits from these schools may be transferable to regular four-year colleges, allowing a student to attend a junior college for a few years, then finish the education at a four-year school. Whether a four-year college accepts these credits, however, is strictly up to the college in question. Some schools are selective as to the credits they will accept. Be sure to check this with the schools beforehand.

Typically, the graduate from a junior or community college can become employed as a junior programmer, computer operator or management trainee.

If you are able to attend and graduate from a four-year college, you will, of course, be in a favored position when seeking employment. The average starting salary currently for a four-year college graduate with a degree in computer science exceeds $20,000 per year.

Graduates with degrees in computer science are in the minority and their ranks cannot fill the manpower requirements of business and industry. As a result, employers who require degrees frequently look for graduates with degrees in fields related to computer science, or graduates from other curriculums who have additional schooling in computer science. An education in mathematics is considered one of the best backgrounds. Business administration and accounting are considered good backgrounds for those who wish to work with business data processing systems. Engineering and the physical sciences provide firm foundations for those who work with scientific computing systems.

Some Unusual Ways to Obtain Your Education and Break Into the Field

This section suggests some unusual methods for obtaining an education and relates stories of others who have received their training and entered the field in some unusual ways.

Congress passed the Comprehensive Employment and Training Act (CETA) for the purpose of providing occupational training for the unemployed. Despite the cutbacks of funding to this program in recent years, anyone who is in need of a job, and can meet certain financial guidelines, may participate in the CETA program. Participants range from individuals who have no high school diploma to those with a master's degree.

Applicants for the CETA program are given a series of aptitude tests. Depending upon the results of these tests, and depending upon the individual's educational background, interest and other factors, the applicant is assigned to a particular skill training program. In a skill training program the individual receives training that prepares him for a new line of work. Participants in a program receive a training allowance, full tuition, books, supplies and in some cases transportation and child care services.

Many branches of the CETA program provide training in the data processing field, frequently by subcontracting the training to a local private data processing school. Whether or not an individual is able to get into one of these computer training programs depends upon all of the factors mentioned earlier, but those who do qualify may receive excellent training free of charge.

CETA programs are usually well advertised locally, but they may not be called CETA. They may go by some other title such as Manpower Program or Job Development Program. If you have difficulty finding your nearest CETA office, look in the phone directory under U.S. Government, Department of Labor. Someone in that department should be able to help you.

One job training program in New England shows much promise for those interested in data processing. The state of Massachusetts is suffering from an acute shortage of qualified data processing personnel. It is also suffering from an overabundance of teachers due to layoffs from a decline in enrollments and fiscal cutbacks.

To help alleviate both of these problems, a group of concerned organizations comprised of the Massachusetts High Technology Council, the Massachusetts Teachers Association and the Massachusetts State Department of Education, combined their efforts and began an experimental training program, aided by funds from the Federal government. This program was designed to re-train unemployed teachers to be programmers. The training was contracted out to a Massachusetts based consulting firm, and consisted of 26 weeks of intensive data processing schooling.

The results from the program were gratifying. Almost all of the 33 teachers who took part in the program were employed by various firms throughout the state. The starting salaries averaged between $18,000 and $19,000 per year, and some went as high as $24,000. These are considered high starting salaries for programmer trainees. One reason these students were able to command such high salaries is because they already possessed four-year college degrees. Also, their past work experiences in teaching provided them with good communications skills which the hiring companies felt would be an asset in their new work in the computer field.

Another group of unemployed individuals is also hoping to be trained shortly for jobs in the field in the state of Massachusetts. The Bay Path Senior Citizen Services,

Inc. is attempting to interest regional computer companies in re-training some of their members to become part-time or full-time data processing employees. This organization has been successful in placing about 22 of their members each month in various jobs around the state. The senior citizens group points out that many of their members have 20, 30, and 40 years of business experience behind them. Some are excellent typists, able to type 60 to 80 words per minute.

To date, the Bay Path Senior Citizens Service has contacted most of the major computer firms in the region. Although no formal program has started yet, all companies have expressed a keen interest in the group and its potential for filling some of the shortages of data processing employees which exist in the state.

Almost every state in the Union can point to a program that it either sponsors or encourages. Moreover, much is also happening at the local level. It only requires taking the time to look for these opportunities.

In Bradenton, Florida, for example, a group of 33 retirees started work immediately with ACS America, a computer software firm, after receiving computer programming training from a free course given by an ACS America subsidiary. This course was specifically designed for the purpose of training retired individuals to work as programmers for ACS. The first group of trainees contained some impressive graduates, including an ex-IBM vice president and several oil company executives. Of course, all of the retirees did not hold such credentials, nor were they required to.

The graduates earn an average of $90 per day. This salary is based on an estimate of how long a given program should take. Regardless of whether a programmer takes more or less time than the estimate for any given program, he is still paid the same amount for that program.

ACS America is extremely pleased with the results of its program and plans to increase its staff of former retirees to 1,000 within the next few years.

Computer programming is an ideal profession for the physically handicapped. A non-profit organization based in Campbell, California, has been formed for the purpose of providing training and employment for the physically handicapped as computer programmers. Disabled Programmers Incorporated (DPI) receives programming contracts from a group of participating companies for various forms of programming work. DPI then custom designs a training program for selected disabled individuals which will meet the demands of the contracting company. Each programmer receives a total of at least four to six months of training before being assigned any company's project. The programmers work either at the client company's site or at the computer installation at DPI.

When a programmer is finished with the contract work for a particular company, that company is given the option of hiring the programmer. If, for some reason, the company chooses not to hire the individual, he is kept on by DPI and assigned to another project.

Much of the contract work performed by DPI programmers is routine maintenance programming and documentation work. It provides excellent training for these disabled persons, many of whom prove to be excellent employees. It also relieves some of the computer personnel shortage experienced by the participating companies, and aids each company in complying with Federal affirmative action guidelines for hiring the handicapped.

For additional information, contact Disabled Programmers Incorporated, One West Campbell Avenue, Campbell, CA 95008.

In Little Rock, Arkansas, an association for the blind is training blind individuals to become programmers. The

Arkansas Enterprise for the Blind (AEB) provides a nine-month course in computer programming for those individuals who qualify. In order to qualify, an applicant for the course is subjected to an extensive one-month evaluation program. This program tests the applicant's typing skills, expertise in mathematics, communications skills, his ability to travel to and from work, and his ability to function in a work environment. Also included is a computer programming aptitude test.

Successful applicants embark on a nine-month training program which includes instruction from audio tape and braille manuals. Students communicate with the computer by using braille terminals and receiving messages from the computer through a voice synthesizer. AEB is proud of the fact that it has a 100% employment rate.

6

Computer Languages Explained

A programmer is an asset to a company's computer operations. The more experience or better education a programmer has in computer languages, the more valuable that programmer will be to the company. Thus, the programmer with both education and experience in computer languages will have the edge in job-hunting.

This chapter is designed to give you an overview of the major languages if you decide to go into programming.

Which Language You Should Study

Computers operate on a language all their own, known as machine language. Programmers can write in this language, and years ago this was often done. Using machine language, though, is a tedious and time-consuming way to program. In this language it is a major task to tell the computer how to add 2 and 2. As a result, more sophisticated or "higher level" programming languages were developed.

These higher level languages enable the programmer to give instructions to the computer in a faster manner because the instructions are closer to standard English.

Hundreds of programming languages have been devised over the years, but not all are in common use today. It will pay us to look at a few of the more common languages to get an idea of their applications, and more importantly, decide which are the best to study.

The determination of which language to study depends upon individual circumstances. For those who are employed by a company, and plan to become a programmer for that company, the answer is simple. Study the language that is used on your company's computer system. For others the answer will not be that simple. In fact, many may have no contact with any computer installation. Perhaps you are in another field or a college student. Or, perhaps you work for a company that has a computer; however, when you inquire as to the language used, you are told there are several. A common response might be that COBOL is used for business applications and FORTRAN for scientific applications.

If you receive such an answer, you must determine which of the two general areas of programming you intend to pursue — business system programming or scientific programming. Each of these areas has its own requirements. Both demand that the programmer use a logical, systematic approach to solve a programming problem, but after this common characteristic, the two categories differ considerably.

Programming for business applications, for which COBOL is the language used most widely, requires familiarity with business systems. Scientific programming does not, but it does make other demands on the programmer.

FORTRAN, for example, is a scientific programming language. As such, it is used for a variety of mathematical applications, varying from simple addition problems to complex problems involving higher mathematics and complicated algorithms. Consequently, many companies will require FORTRAN programmers to have a strong mathematical background. As an example, a master's degree in mathematics might be required. If you do not have such a background you may find it difficult to get started in the area of scientific programming. This is not to say that you could not handle many FORTRAN problems without this background, or that there are not FORTRAN programmers who do not have degrees in math or engineering. But it is fair to say you may run into this type of employment requirement if you attempt to pursue a career in this area. (FORTRAN will be explained in greater detail later in this chapter).

If you currently work for a company that has a computer, the question of which language to study has probably been answered for you. If you are not in such a position, the question becomes more difficult to answer. No one can predict your future. You can't predict where you will be one year or five years from now in your data processing career. However, some of the best languages to study, based upon the languages used most often today, are listed below:

Business Languages	**Scientific Languages**
COBOL	FORTRAN
RPG II	BASIC
BASIC	PASCAL
PASCAL	PL/1
PL/1	

A few languages are listed in both columns because some have characteristics which make them adaptable to either business or scientific applications.

COBOL

COBOL stands for COmmon Business Oriented Language. Hearing the word "COBOL" would proably ring a bell in the heads of millions of Americans, including those who know little or nothing about the field of data processing. "Doesn't that have something to do with computers?" might be a typical response. There's a good reason for this. COBOL is the most common business data processing language in use today. It was invented in 1960 in an effort to produce a programming language that was as near to the English language as possible. The reasons for this are obvious. It would be easier for programmers to communicate with the computer and it would be easier to train new programmers. A statement such as MULTIPLY PRICE TIMES QUANTITY is an example of a typical COBOL statement.

COBOL is a high level, procedural language which has many advantages. In addition to the aforementioned English language type format, COBOL has the ability to handle files of data more easily and with greater flexibility than many other languages. It is compatible when moving from one computer system to another, and its construction allows a single large program to be broken down into segments so that several programmers can work on the same program simultaneously.

A COBOL program is broken down into four separate parts or divisions known as the IDENTIFICATION division, ENVIRONMENT division, DATA division, and PROCEDURE division.

The IDENTIFICATION division is a small set of statements serving simply to identify the program name, and perhaps date written, company name and programmer's name.

The ENVIRONMENT division is comprised of two

subsections: the CONFIGURATION section and the INPUT-OUTPUT section. The CONFIGURATION section is used to describe the type of computer on which the program is run. The INPUT-OUTPUT section is used to describe which input and output devices are being accessed. It may indicate, for example, that data is read in from a computer tape file and that data is printed out on a printer.

The DATA division is also comprised of two subsections: the FILE section and the WORKING STORAGE section. The FILE section gives a detailed description of each file used by the program, including a description of the data in each file. The WORKING STORAGE section defines data that is not found in any of the input or output records. For example, an account number field called ACCOUNT-NUMBER may lie in a record which is read into the program. This field would be described in the FILE section. The programmer may create a field named TOTAL into which he adds the balance due for each record read in. This field would be described in the WORKING STORAGE section.

The PROCEDURE division encompasses the real heart of the program. It specifies the logical steps necessary for the program to perform its task. Included are calculations, input and output operations, logical decisions and data handling commands.

```
 IDENTIFICATION DIVISION.
 PROGRAM-ID.    PRTLIST.
 AUTHOR.        PETE CARRON.
 DATE-WRITTEN.  09/01/81.

* THIS PROGRAM PRINTS A LIST OF ALL ACCOUNTS

 ENVIRONMENT DIVISION.
 CONFIGURATION SECTION.
 SOURCE-COMPUTER. IBM-S34.
 OBJECT-COMPUTER. IBM-S34.

 INPUT-OUTPUT SECTION.
 FILE-CONTROL.
     SELECT ACCOUNTFILE
           ASSIGN TO DISK-ACFILE.
     SELECT PRINTOUT
           ASSIGN TO PRINTER-PRT.

 DATA DIVISION.
 FILE SECTION.
 FD ACCOUNTFILE
       RECORD CONTAINS 30 CHARACTERS
       LABEL RECORDS ARE STANDARD
       DATA RECORD IS ACCOUNTFILE.
 01  ACCOUNTFILE.
     05  ACCOUNTNUMBER-INPUT     PICTURE X(5).
     05  NAME-INPUT              PICTURE X(25).
 FD  PRINTOUT
       RECORD CONTAINS 132 CHARACTERS
       LABEL RECORDS ARE OMITTED
       DATARECORD IS PRINTLINE.
 01  PRINTLINE.
     05 ACCOUNTNUMBER-REPORT     PICTURE X(5).
     05 FILLER                   PICTURE X(5).
     05 NAME-REPORT              PICTURE X(25).

 WORKING-STORAGE SECTION.
 01  PROGRAM-INDICATORS.
     05  ARE-THERE-MORE-RECORDS  PICTURE X(3) VALUE 'YES'.

 PROCEDURE DIVISION.
 A000-CREATE-ACCOUNT-LIST
     OPEN INPUT  ACCOUNTFILE.
          OUTPUT PRINTOUT.
     READ ACCOUNTFILE
```

COBOL Program - part 1

```
          AT END
             MOVE 'NO' TO ARE-THERE-MORE-RECORDS.
    PERFORM A001-WRITE-PRINT-LINE
          UNTIL ARE-THERE-MORE-RECORDS = 'NO'.
    CLOSE ACCOUNTFILE
          PRINTOUT.
    STOP RUN.

A001-WRITE-PRINT-LINE.
    MOVE SPACES TO PRINTLINE.
    MOVE ACCOUNTNUMBER-INPUT TO ACCOUNTNUMBER-REPORT.
    MOVE NAME-INPUT TO NAME-REPORT.
    WRITE PRINTLINE
          AFTER ADVANCING 2 LINES.
    READ ACCOUNTFILE
          AT END
             MOVE 'NO ' TO ARE-THERE-MORE RECORDS.
```

COBOL Program - part 2

RPG II

RPG II is a newer version of a language originally called RPG which stands for Report Program Generator.

RPG II is not a procedural language like COBOL or FORTRAN. It is a business systems, problem-oriented language. That is, it is designed so the programmer can feed certain information into a program, on one of five different specification sheets, thereby "telling the program what he wants." From the information that is fed in, the computer generates its own program. This is a great oversimplification of the language, but fundamentally it is what RPG II is all about.

The five types of specification sheets used in the language are FILE DESCRIPTION specifications, FILE EXTENSION specifications, INPUT specifications, CALCULATION specifications and OUTPUT specifications.

FILE DESCRIPTION specification sheets define the attributes of each of the input and output files used by the program. They describe the size of the records in each file and tell what input or output device the file is stored on. For example, they may show that a file called MASTER is 100 positions long and is stored on a computer disk file.

INPUT specification sheets define in detail what is in each of the input files just described on the FILE DESCRIPTION specifications. They might show that a person's account number is in positions 1 to 5 of the records in the file called MASTER, and that the person's name is in positions 6 to 25 of the same record, etc.

FILE EXTENSION specifications are not used as frequently as the other types of specifications sheets. They are most often used to define "tables" within a program. A table is a device that is used to look up, or search for information. For example, a table of the 50 state abbreviation codes (e.g. CA = California) may be stored in a program. This table would be defined on the FILE EXTENSION specifications.

CALCULATION specifications are used to do calculations. You can add, subtract, multiply and divide in RPG II. Some machines have the ability to take square roots, but after that you can't do much more from a mathematical standpoint. There are no commands to allow you to find sines or cosines, or raise a number to a power. These specifications are used for other functions also, but performance of mathematical calculations is their primary purpose.

OUTPUT specification sheets describe in detail the output for each of the output files that was described on the FILE DESCRIPTION specifications. If you are printing a report, you can tell the program to print an individual's account number starting at print position 2 on the printer, and print his name starting at print position 10, etc.

Since RPG II is not a procedural language, its logic is completely different from that of languages such as COBOL or FORTRAN. Due to this difference, some programmers have difficulty learning the language. Once mastered, however, it is an excellent language. And most important of all, it is used on many of today's small business computers.

```
H                                             1
F* THIS PROGRAM PRINTS A LISTING OF ALL ACCOUNTS WITH
F* BALANCES OVER 90 DAYS OLD
FFILEIN  IP  F 128 128 05AI       1 DISK
FREPORT  O   F 132 132      OF      PRINTER
IFILEIN  AA  01
I                                                1   50ACCTNO
I                                                6  25 NAME
I                                               26  322CURR
I                                               33  392OVER30
I                                               40  462OVER60
I                                               47  532OVER90
I                                               54  602OVR120
I                                               61  660LASTPA
C   01                 SETOF                              20
C   01        OVER90   COMP 0                         20
C   01N20     OVR120   COMP 0                         20
C*
C   01                 Z-ADD0           TOTAL    72
C   01        CURR     ADD  TOTAL       TOTAL
C   01        CURR30   ADD  TOTAL       TOTAL
C   01        OVER60   ADD  TOTAL       TOTAL
C   01        OVER90   ADD  TOTAL       TOTAL
C   01        OVR120   ADD  TOTAL       TOTAL
OREPORT  H    201    1P
O       OR           OF
O                                     8 'PROG01'
O                          UDATE Y   20
O                                    64 'ACCOUNTS OVER'
O                                    75 '90 DAYS OLD'
O                                   124 'PAGE'
O                          PAGE  Z  130
O        H    2      1P
O       OR           OF
O                                    21 'ACCT NO          NAME'
O                                    52 'CURR        OVER 30'
O                                    77 'OVER 60       OVER 90'
O                                    99 'OVER 120     TOTAL'
O                                   112 'LAST PAY'
O        D    1      01 20
O                          ACCTNO     8
O                          NAME      30
O                          CURR   J  42
O                          OVER30J   54
O                          OVER60J   66
O                          OVER90J   78
O                          OVR120J   90
O                          TOTAL JB 102
O                          LASTPAY  112
```

RPG II Program

FORTRAN

FORTRAN stands for FORmula TRANslation. It is a mathematical, or scientific programming language. Actually FORTRAN is the scientific counterpart of COBOL in that it is also a powerful, procedural language.

FORTRAN was invented in 1956 and still stands today as one of the most commonly used and most powerful scientific languages. Although it can be used for business applications, such use is less common.

Many of the symbols and commands used in FORTRAN resemble their real life counterpart in the field of mathematics. Here again we see a similarity between FORTRAN and COBOL. COBOL uses many English language-like commands while FORTRAN will use many mathematically compatible symbols and commands, and some of the more common ones appear on the next list.

+	Addition
-	Subtraction
/	Division
=	Equal to
SIN	Compute sine of angle
COS	Compute cosine of angle

Additional abbreviations for mathematical functions are listed below.

*	Multiplication
**	Exponentiation (raising a number to a power)
SQRT	Compute the square root
.EQ.	Equal to
.NE.	Not equal to
.GT.	Greater than
.LT.	Less than
.GE.	Greater than or equal to
.LE.	Less than or equal to

In addition to the mathematical symbols just listed, there are other commands needed to tell the program what to do. The various types of statements used in FORTRAN are divided into these four categories:

1. INPUT/OUTPUT statements - These statements control movement of data between the program and various input and output devices. They can be used, for example, to tell the program when to read a record from a file or when to print a line on a report. READ and WRITE are two examples of such statements.
2. SPECIFICATION statements - Specification statements describe to the program the types of data with which it is working. For example, a field called AMOUNT may be seven digits long and have two decimal positions. The program must be told this to use the field successfully.
3. ARITHMETIC statements - These are used to perform mathematical calculations. Samples of these statements were just listed.
4. CONTROL statements - Control statements tell the program what steps to do next. GOTO is a typical example, and is used to tell the program to go to another point in the program. CALL is a statement that calls a subroutine (a small program in itself) into the main program.

```
C*************************************************************
C THIS PROGRAM CALCULATES THE ROWING SPEED FOR EACH MEMBER
C OF A ROWING TEAM, AND PRINTS FINAL TOTALS OF THE AVERAGE
C SPEED OF ALL THE MEMBERS, AND THE HIGHEST ROWING SPEED
C OF ANY ONE MEMBER
C*************************************************************
      SPEED = 0.0
      HISPED = 0.0
      TOTSPD = 0.0
      ICOUNT = 0.0
      COUNT = 0.0
      AVERGE = 0.0
C*****
   10 READ (5,71) CURRNT,ZZZZ,U
   20 READ (5,72) RNAME1,RNAME2,RNAME3,UPDOWN,TIME
C*****
      IF (RNAME3 .EQ. ZZZZ) GO TO 100
      IF (UPDOWN .EQ. U) GO TO 40
      SPEED = (1/(TIME/3600.0)) - CURRNT
      GO TO 50
   40 SPEED = (1/(TIME/3600.0)) + CURRNT
   50 WRITE (6,73) RNAME1,RNAME2,RNAME3,SPEED
      IF (SPEED .LT. HISPED) GO TO 60
      HISPED = SPEED
   60 TOTSPD = TOTSPD + SPEED
      ICOUNT = ICOUNT + 1
      GO TO 20
  100 COUNT = FLOAT (ICOUNT)
      AVERGE = (TOTSPD/COUNT)
      WRITE (6,74) AVERGE
      WRITE (6,75) HISPED
      STOP
C*************************************************************
   72 FORMAT (3A4,A1,F3.0)
   71 FORMAT (F3.1,A4,A1)
   73 FORMAT (3A4,5X,F4.2,2X,'MILES PER HOUR')
   74 FORMAT (///,'THE AVERAGE SPEED IS',3X,F5.2,3X,'MPH')
   75 FORMAT (///,'THE HIGHEST SPEED IS',3X,F5.2,3X,'MPH')
C*************************************************************
      END
```

FORTRAN Program

BASIC

BASIC stands for Beginners All purpose Symbolic Instruction Code. For people who are home computer enthusiasts, the word BASIC will sound very familiar. The BASIC language is currently used on more home computers than any other language. This language was originally invented for use on time-sharing computer systems. Although it is still widely used for that purpose today, its use has been expanded to other areas. BASIC is now used on many small business computer systems.

BASIC is a procedural language which is similar to, but not as powerful as, FORTRAN. Although it is not considered a high-powered language, it is more than adequate for most small business applications. The language is listed as both a business systems language and a scientific language. Indeed, it is very versatile and also one of the easiest languages to learn. Listed below are some of the commands used for mathematical functions.

+	Addition
-	Subtraction
*	Multiplication
/	Division
↑	Exponentiation
=	Equal to
<	Less than
>	Greater than
<=	Less than or equal to
>=	Greater than or equal to
<>	Not equal to
SIN	Compute sine of angle
COS	Compute cosine of angle
TAN	Compute tangent of angle
ABS	Compute the absolute value of
SQR	Compute the square root of

In addition to those listed, other commands are needed to instruct the program to perform various functions. Statements are used to define variables in the program. Statements such as LET A = 1, or LET R = (X*Y) are two examples. Statements are needed to read data, such as READ B, or INPUT A1. Statements are needed to write data, such as PRINT B, or PRINT C + (M/L). And statements are needed to make decisions and define various conditions, such as IF A > B GOTO 120.

If there are any drawbacks to the language at all, it is simply that there are many versions of the language. As it is used on more and more computer systems, each computer manufacturer appears to come up with its own version. There is ADVANCED BASIC, EXTENDED BASIC, BENTON HARBOR BASIC, SUPER BASIC, BASIC BASIC, etc. However, this should not discourage anyone from learning the language, for ninety-percent of the commands will still be compatible from one machine to another.

```
100 REM  THIS PROGRAM COMPUTES THE VALUE OF X, USING ONE
110 REM  OF FOUR FORMULAS, SELECTED BY THE OPERATOR
120 PRINT 'ENTER VALUE OF LONGEST DIMENSION- A'
130 READ A
140 PRINT 'ENTER VALUE OF SHORTEST DIMENSION- B'
150 READ B
160 PRINT 'ENTER MAXIMUM NUMBER OF ITEMS TO BE USED'
170 READ C
180 PRINT 'ENTER METHOD YOU WISH TO USE TO CALCULATE X'
190 PRINT 'METHOD 1,2,3 OR 4'
200 READ Y
210   IF Y=1 GO TO 300
220   IF Y=2 GO TO 400
230   IF Y=3 GO TO 500
240   IF Y=4 GO TO 600
300 REM  THIS SECTION IS USED TO CALCULATE X BY METHOD 1
310   IF (A/B)<2 THEN 330
320   IF (A/B)=>2 THEN 350
330 Z=(C*2)↑2
340 GO TO 900
350 Z=(C*2)↑3
360 GO TO 900
400 REM  THIS SECTION IS USED TO CALCULATE X BY METHOD 2
410   IF (A/B)<2 THEN 430
420   IF (A/B)=>2 THEN 450
430 Z=(C*3)↑3
440 GO TO 900
450 Z=(C*3)↑4
460 GO TO 900
500 REM  THIS SECTION IS USED TO CALCULATE X BY METHOD 3
510   IF (A/B)<2 THEN 530
520   IF (A/B)=>2 THEN 550
530 Z=(C*4)↑4
540 GO TO 900
550 Z=(C*4)↑5
560 GO TO 900
600 REM  THIS SECTION IS USED TO CALCULATE X BY METHOD 4
610   IF (A/B)<2 THEN 630
620   IF (A/B)=>2 THEN 650
630 Z=(C*5)↑5
640 GO TO 900
650 Z=(C*5)↑6
660 GO TO 900
900 X=3*SQR(Z)
910 PRINT 'THE VALUE OF X IS',X
920 PRINT 'WHICH HAS BEEN CALCULATED BY METHOD',Y
930 END
```

BASIC Program

PASCAL

PASCAL was invented in 1971 with the dual intention of developing a language that could be used to teach computer programming as a systematic discipline as well as to provide a language that would be reliable and efficient on the computers that were presently available. This language is presented here because its use has increased dramatically in recent years. It is presently taught in many computer science curricula, and appears to be one of the languages of the future.

The PASCAL language has one outstanding feature that has helped it gain popularity. It is one of the few languages that enables the programmer to find coding errors quickly. To understand this feature better we could look closer at the meaning of the word "compile," and the meaning of the ever-popular programming buzz word "bug."

There are two types of errors, or bugs, which the programmer may find in his program. One is a bug that the computer itself can detect, while the other is a bug that only the programmer can detect.

The abbreviated dictionary of data processing terms in Chapter 2 defines the word "compile" as, "To convert a source program (a program which a programmer has written) into an object program (a program which the machine understands)."At the same time this conversion occurs, a list of error messages is printed which tells the programmer what errors are in his program. Some typical error messages might look like these:

"A subroutine called SUBRO1 has been called by the program, but cannot be found."

"Your are attempting to use the operation code ADD with alphabetic data instead of numeric data."

"Your GOTO command is not followed by a legitimate statement number."

Error messages such as these tell the programmer he has errors in his program because he has not strictly adhered to the rules of the programming language in which he is writing. Upon seeing these error messages, or compiler errors, as they are called, the programmer makes corrections to his program until it finally compiles error free.

Unfortunately, getting a program to compile error free is only part of the job. The program will compile and run once is has met all of the strict rules of the programming language in which it is written. but if a programmer makes an error and tells the program to add federal income tax to gross wages, instead of telling it to subtract federal income tax from gross wages, the program has no way of knowing this operation is incorrect. It will always dutifully add taxes to gross wages, and arrive at a net wages figure that is greater than the gross wages.

The programmer spends the majority of his time correcting errors of this type; that is, the type which the compiler cannot detect for him. The PASCAL language, however, is so designed that the number of errors that can get past the compiler is held to a minimum. As a result, the programmer is aided in writing a program error-free.

PASCAL, like BASIC, can be used as a business systems language or a scientific language.

Listed here are some of the symbols and commands used for mathematical operations.

+	Addition
-	Subtraction
*	Multiplication
/	Division
=	Equal to
<>	Not equal to
<	Less than
>	Greater than

< =	Less than or equal to
> =	Greater than or equal to
SIN	Compute sine of angle
COS	Compute cosine of angle
SQRT	Compute the square root of
ABS	Compute the absolute value of

```
PROGRAM PYRL14 (INPUT,OUTPUT,MASTFILE);
{ASSUMING GROSS HAS BEEN CALCULATED, CALCULATE NET PAYROLL}
{FOR ALL EMPLOYEES IN A DISK FILE CALLED "PYRLMAST.FIL"    }
{WHICH IS LOCATED ON DISK DRIVE "E:"  BY JOHN DAHNERT       }
CONST
   FICARATE = 0.0665;
   FEDWHRATE = 0.20;
   FICALIMIT = 29700.00;
TYPE
   MASTER = RECORD
               GROSS    , FICA     , FEDWH    , NET      ,
               YTDGROSS, TXBLEGROSS                          : REAL;
            END;
VAR
   MASTFILE : FILE OF MASTER;

PROCEDURE FICATXBLE;
   VAR
      OVERLIMIT : REAL;
   BEGIN
      WITH MASTFILE^DO
         BEGIN
            YTDGROSS := YTDGROSS + GROSS;
            IF YTDGROSS >= FICALIMIT THEN
               BEGIN
                  OVERLIMIT := YTDGROSS - FICALIMIT;
                  TXBLEGROSS := GROSS -OVERLIMIT
               END
            ELSE
               TXBLEGROSS := GROSS
         END
   END; {OF PROCEDURE FICATXBLE}

BEGIN {MAIN PROGRAM}
   RESET (MASTFILE, 'E:PYRLMAST.FIL');
   REWRITE (MASTFILE, 'E:PYRLMAST.FIL');
   WHILE NOT EOF(MASTFILE) DO
      BEGIN
         IF MASTFILE^.YTDGROSS < FICALIMIT THEN
            FICATXBLE
         ELSE
            MASTFILE^.TXBLEGROSS := 0.00;
         WITH MASTFILE^DO
            BEGIN
               FICA:= TXBLEGROSS * FICARATE;  {CALC TAXES}
               FEDWH := GROSS * FEDWHRATE;

               NET := GROSS - FICA;           {CALC NET PAY}
               NET := NET - FEDWH;
            END;
         PUT (MASTFILE)
      END;
   CLOSE (MASTFILE,LOCK)
END.
```

PASCAL Program

Other Languages

The more common programming languages in use today have just been covered. It is interesting, though, to look at a few of the others. All languages fall into one of five categories as listed below.

1. Algorithmic and Procedural Languages - This category includes languages that are written in a step-by-step procedural fashion, something on the order of READ this, GOTO there, PRINT that, etc. FORTRAN and COBOL are both procedural languages.
2. Time-sharing Languages - These are used in time-sharing computer systems where many users access the same computer at the same time, from different computer terminals.
3. Process Control Languages - Process control languages control various industrial processes. One example is the control of the heating and cooling units in a building for the purpose of minimizing energy usage. Another example is the control of a machine in a manufacturing process to produce a certain shaped object.
4. Simulation Languages - These are used to enable the computer to simulate some physical system or phenomenon, such as the simulation of a particular chemical process.
5. List Processing Languages - These languages are used strictly for convenience and for the manipulation of data. They are used for widely varying applications such as linguistic analysis (analyzing languages) and information retrieval.

Now look at some of the other languages. Even their names are fascinating.

QUICKTRAN - This is a time-sharing language, similar to FORTRAN. One of QUICKTRAN's strong points is that it gives the programmer complete control over his program, allowing easy addition of, or change to, parameters (variables) and program statements.

ALGOL - ALGOL stands for ALGOrithmic Language, and was designed as a language that could easily express an algorithm. It is used primarily for scientific purposes and is similar to FORTRAN.

LISP - LISP is an acronym for LISt Processing language, and is the list processing language from which most other list processing languages have been developed.

LOGO - The growing popularity of personal computers (microcomputers) - especially in schools and homes - is increasing the use of a "beginner's" language, called LOGO. In very simple terms, this comparatively slow language divides a problem into small segments or "procedures" and allows the computer to build a "vocabulary" of new words or concepts. In the years ahead, LOGO's primary contribution to this field will be to introduce computers to a greater number of people than ever before, despite its limited use in the business world.

CAL - CAL stands for Conversational Algebraic Language. It is a time-sharing language which is used for mathematical applications.

SNOBOL - SNOBOL is an acronym for StriNg Oriented symBOLic language. It is a list processing language often used for word processing and linguistic problems.

PL/1 - PL/1 stands for Programming Language 1. This is a versatile language that can be used for business or scientific applications. It incorporates some of the features of both COBOL and FORTRAN. PL/1 is particularly well suited for *specific* applications and it can be easily modified to meet many different needs.

COMIT - Also a list processing language. It was developed primarily for use in studies of mechanical translations of the human language.

APL - APL stands for A Programming Language. It is a procedural language that has some unique characteristics, one being its ability to perform certain mathematical manipulations by using far fewer statements as compared to other languages.

APT - APT stands for Automatic Programmed Tools. This is a process control language designed specifically for the purpose of controlling machine tools.

JOVIAL - JOVIAL is an acronym for Jules' Own Version of the International Algorithmic Language. It was developed by a man named Jules (who else) Schwartz. This is a procedural language developed from the ALGOL language.

JOSS - JOSS stands for Johniac Open Shop System. It is a time-sharing language, similar to some other algebraic languages, and is used primarily for solving mathematical calculations that require immediate results.

COGO - COGO is a process control language developed for use by civil engineers and is based upon civil engineering technology.

One final word of advice before you select your computer language: Take the time to review your career objectives *before* you decide on the language(s) you plan to learn. Your future job opportunities (and satisfaction) may depend on it!

7 The Many Applications of Computers

Once you break into the computer field you will find a profession that has limitless horizons. The capabilities and uses of computers appear boundless, and they make an interesting story, the beginning of which goes back many years.

The field of data processing began with the invention of the abacus over 5,000 years ago, but not until the year 1833 did a machine appear which even faintly resembled a computer. In that year, a man name Charles P. Babbage invented a mechanical calculating device that incorporated many of the ideas we see in today's modern computers. Finally, in 1946, the first all-electronic computer was completed. This machine was called ENIAC, for Electronic Numerical Integrator and Computer. It was a monstrous machine that weighed 30 tons and contained 18,000 vacuum tubes.

When Charles Babbage set out to build his mechanical calculator in the 1830's, his goal was to build a machine that could perform one calculation in one second. How primitive that sounds compared to the machines that followed in later years! From the invention of ENIAC until today, the speed of computers has increased dramatically.

ENIAC was able to multiply two 10-digit numbers in 1/40 of a second.

By the year 1953, machines could multiply two 10-digit numbers in 1/2,000 of a second.

By 1959, with the invention of the transistor, machines could multiply two 10-digit numbers in 1/100,000 of a second, and computer printer speeds had been increased so that some printers could print at a rate of 600 lines per minute.

By 1964, computers could perform 2,500,000 additions per second.

By 1967, some of our largest computers could perform additions at the rate of 16,000,000 per second, and print at speeds of several thousand lines per minute.

Today, the figures are even more impressive. But speed is only part of the story. The range of applications for computers is just as remarkable. To list a few of these applications, we find that computers are used to:

print paychecks,

blend steel mixtures,

maintain financial account balances,

guide missiles,

keep track of orders, sales and inventories,

mix colors for the textile industry,

save large amounts of energy and money by use of computerized energy management systems in industrial buildings,

blend dog foods,

ENIAC, the first all-electronic computer

send a man to the moon,
perform every banking application,
search for a new planet,
play games,
perform seismic analysis to anticipate volcanic eruptions,
teach students,
print reports with laser printers at the incredible speed of 20,000 lines per minute,
write music,
sort information in any order,
track satellites,
print bills, mailing labels and purchase orders,
draw graphs,
maintain medical records,
solve crimes,
and perform many other tasks.

That's quite an assorted list of applications, and most have been added in just the past few decades. All of these uses for computers, and more, can be organized into three groups.

Computers in Business

Some computer uses in the business world are obvious. We all know that computers prepare our paycheck, print the hospital's bill and maintain our bank account balance. But the range of applications for computers in business extends far beyond these areas. There are computer applications in many companies that touch every facet of their operations, including:

order entry,
accounts receivable,
accounts payable,
payroll,
general ledger,
personnel,
purchasing,
sales,
inventory,
product testing,
market sampling,
materials handling,
production control and scheduling,
project scheduling,
research and development,
and management reporting.

The computer is used to store names and addresses and other information concerning customers, vendors, employees, salesmen, inventory items and orders.

The computer is used to print purchase orders, customer's orders, invoices, statements, credit memos, credit and collection reports, aged trial balances, sales analysis reports, packing slips, vouchers, accounts payable checks, payroll checks, profit and loss statements, balance sheets, routing sheets, production control and scheduling reports, shipment forecasts, inventory reports and other management and information reports.

Up to four computer workstations can be supported by a disk storage unit for the IBM Datamaster small business system.

The following stories describe some real life computer applications in business . . .

A new computer installation is serving the 72-county welfare system of the state of Wisconsin. Prior to the installation of this system, it required weeks to determine whether an applicant was eligible for aid. Now it takes only

One of IBM's largest central processing units, the IBM 3033 (center)

hours. This has been accomplished by the installation of a central computer system linked by phone lines to 18 remote terminals. In addition to the drastically reduced turnaround time to determine eligibility, the new computer installation has saved the state $10 million per year in clerical costs.

A public utility company in Missouri is using computers to help project their future financial needs enabling them to file for rate changes well in advance of their actual needs for cash. The computer system at Missouri Power and Light Company is able to prepare data for rate cases, even as the cases are being presented in public utility commission hearings.

The vice president of a large glass container manufacturer in California is extremely happy with his new computer system. When he arrives at the office early in the morning, the first thing he does is query his new computer terminal for production data from the previous day's operations at twelve different manufacturing facilities. He obtains immediate response from each location on total units produced, total units packed, tonnage of raw material used and other vital statistics. His new information processing network not only ties together twelve manufacturing plants but also interlinks thirteen sales offices, using a total of 102 computer terminals. The most important benefit of the system, he comments, is the availability of up-to-the-minute data which has proved valuable in early problem identification. This data helps management make proper management decisions more quickly.

The IBM 6670 Information Distributor can be used to collect, print and reproduce information from remote locations.

An Arizona-based hotel chain recently installed a computer system that links together over 2,600 of their hotels in places as nearby as Phoenix and as far away as Limerick, Ireland. The new system prepares accurate reservations for travelers, regardless of where they live in the world. Prior to the installation of the system, it required two days to confirm a reservation for a room in the U.S. from a location in Europe. Today, it takes 30 seconds.

Honeywell's Page Printing System (PPS)
This free-standing, magnetic tape-to-hard copy system offers printed output, cut and stacked, ready for binding.

IBM 3800 Laser Printer

This high-speed, general-purpose, non-impact printer uses electrophotographic and laser technologies to achieve very high speeds—as high as 20,000 lines per minute. It is especially useful for large-volume, standard-form applications.

Computers in Science and Engineering

Computers in science and engineering provide some of the most fascinating applications of computers imaginable. They are used in virtually every field of science and engineering, including, among others:

electrical engineering,
chemical engineering,
industrial engineering,
civil engineering,
mechanical engineering,
astronomy,
chemistry,
physics,
geology,
mathematics,
metallurgy,
oceanography,
energy research,
nuclear research,
and space research.

Computers perform measurements and calculations, draw graphs, blueprints and maps, perform automated analyses of stresses, chemical compositions and colors, take counts, determine routes and schedule traffic.

Computers control electric power plants and water utilities, control production facilities in oil refineries and search for oil and gas wells.

Computers study the sun, monitor tornados, predict the paths of hurricanes, forecast the weather, track comets and perform seismic exploration.

Computers track satellites, guide rockets and control complex switching systems for communications networks.

One of the most widely recognized uses of computers in science is that of guiding and controlling spacecraft. For example, computers were used extensively in April, 1981 when the space shuttle Columbia completed its successful space mission after orbiting the earth 36 times. The mission was accomplished exactly as planned. Only those knowledgeable in the mechanics behind the operation can appreciate the amazing assortment of data processing hardware and software (computer programs) that went into making the mission a success.

Behind the scenes was the largest array of computers ever used for any space mission. These machines were applied to monitor the countdown prior to launching, to guide the shuttle during its space flight, to monitor all systems during the entire flight, to aid the two astronauts with system management, and were prepared to guide the craft back to earth in the event of a serious system failure.

On board the craft were five separate guidance and control computers, each weighing about 55 pounds. These were far different from the first all-electronic computer (which weighed 30 tons) of 35 years earlier and much more sophisticated than the computers that were used for the first moon landing twelve years earlier. Advances have been considerable in just the past two or three decades. These more recent machines operated 40 times faster and had five times the memory capacity of those used for the first moon voyage.

On the ground was another sophisticated arrangement of computers. Prior to launch time the launch countdown was monitored by the Launch Processing System at Kennedy Space Center. This system comprised eight launch processing sites. Each site contained up to 40 minicomputers (small computers). During flight, the space shuttle's every move was monitored by three large computers at the Johnson Space Center.

Astronaut John Young, commander of the first Shuttle Orbiter, in the cabin of "Columbia"

The weather is always an interesting topic. It's even more interesting when computers are involved, as they have been from the day they were first invented.

The story begins in 1922 when a man named Lewis Richardson developed the first mathematical technique for predicting the weather. He assigned numbers to various elements of the weather such as temperature, humidity and barometric pressure. In 1946, a scientist at Princeton University named John Von Neuman put the first computers to work in an attempt to predict the weather. By 1955, we were receiving regularly scheduled weather forecasts generated by computer.

Of course, weather forecasts are not as accurate as we would like them to be and there are a number of reasons. First, and most important, there are many variables involved in predicting the weather. As one scientist quipped, "A tornado in Kansas may have been caused by a butterfly flapping his wings in Bermuda a week before." Although this may be somewhat far-fetched, it is a fact that weather patterns at widely different locations around the globe do have an effect on each other. To assimilate the necessary information from various points around the globe, scientists gather data from some 10,000 weather monitoring stations around the world. These stations include ground based observation points, weather balloons, aircraft, ships and weather satellites.

Next are the problems of transmitting, analyzing and reporting on all this data. This requires the use of very powerful computers, running complex programs.

Despite all the problems involved, however, advances in the field are being made constantly, as more and more powerful computers are produced. Today, computers are used not only to help predict the weather, but also to track tornados, monitor and analyze the activity of the sun, track meteorites to predict their point of contact with the earth, predict the path of hurricanes and simulate various atmospheric conditions (with these models, we can hope to predict weather years in advance, or predict the effects of air pollution on our weather).

Astronomy is another science which has benefited greatly by the advent of computers. One of the most useful applications in astronomy is that of tracking the planets and the stars. Moreover, many stars are so faint they cannot be seen by the human eye even with our most powerful telescopes. In such cases, time lapse photographs are taken of these stars, and the photos are studied. Even then, many stars still appear as faint, indistinguishable blotches of light. Scientists can now use computers to aid in their quest. Hyron Spinrad, an astronomer at Berkeley, has successfully identified a giant galaxy by using a computerized "image tube scanner" system. The computer's role was to enhance the image by eliminating extraneous light and by supplementing light from the image. This galaxy, designated as 3C123 on star maps, was one of the most distant objects of its kind ever discovered, being some eight billion light years away from earth.

The planet Pluto was discovered in 1930, but the possibility that such a planet existed was suspected for many years prior to its actual discovery. These suspicions originated from observations of irregularities in the orbits of Neptune and Uranus. Work began to uncover the reasons for these irregularities, and the discovery of Pluto resulted.

Today, scientists are looking for a 10th planet. This time they are using computers to aid in the search. Although it is now only an hypothesis, scientists at the U.S. Naval Observatory suspect there may be a 10th planet, of perhaps two to five times the mass of the earth, orbiting beyond Neptune. Aiding in their search is an IBM computer which is capable of computing a 400-year orbit for a planet in two hours.

At Mount St. Helens in the state of Washington, seismologists are using computers for a different purpose. Thirteen monitoring stations near Mount St. Helens and 70 other monitoring stations throughout the state are being used to continuously collect seismic data. This data is immediately sent to a central computer system at the University of Washington in Seattle, where it is collected and analyzed at the rate of 100 samples of data per second from each station. The computer is able to distinguish between unwanted signals such as those which originate from heavy truck traffic and true ground movement signals.

Seismologists are using the data to pinpoint the center of seismic movements and help predict the future occurrence of quakes or volcanic eruptions. In this case, the computer is in an online, realtime environment. This simply means that a particular program is running constantly (24 hours per day) and is responsible for the analysis, dissemination and/or processing of the input data.

Computers are also helping scientists with one of the greatest problems modern man has ever faced: the energy crisis.

The Laboratory for Laser Energetics at the University of Rochester in Rochester, New York, is using a 12-trillion-watt laser beam system to fire fuel pellets to a temperature of 50 million degrees. These incomprehensible power levels and temperatures are reached in an effort to study the feasibility of using controlled thermonuclear fusion as a source of power to help alleviate the energy crisis.

The results of experiments such as these generate huge amounts of data which can only be handled by large computers. As a result, the Laboratory for Laser Energetics is using a powerful Control Data Corp. computer system to process the data from its experiments and to manipulate volumes of complex mathematical equations involved in such an undertaking.

Other Applications of Computers

COMPUTER GRAPHICS has been around for a long time, but it is a term seldom heard until recent years. Today, some form of computer graphics is used in almost every area in which computers are used.

Computer graphics is the process of communicating with a computer pictorially; that is, with pictures or drawings rather than letters and numbers.

The benefit of computer graphics can be readily appreciated by anyone who has ever attempted to decipher a land deed. This deed might read as follows: "Beginning at a stake in the ground at the corner of the properties currently owned by John J. Ubrinthal and Hattie R. Wackenbush, thence 90 degrees westerly by 46.2 degrees southerly to a point 432 feet 7 inches to a marker, thence 20.2 degrees north for a distance of 116 feet 2 inches to a point . . ." There can only be one thought of anyone who reads such a description, "A map would be a lot easier to understand." And so it would. By means of computer-graphics, this map, or any other, can be easily constructed.

The two most common tools for producing maps or other drawings or pictures are the cathode ray tube and the computer-controlled mechanical plotting board. A variety of devices are used by an operator to communicate with the computer. The "light pen" is a hand-held device shaped like a pen or pencil, and can be used to communicate with a CRT display by "drawing" lines on the display tube. "Electronic tablets" can also be used. These devices provide a flat writing surface, somewhat like a notepad, on which the operator can "write" commands to the computer.

In certain computer graphics applications, the operator can communicate "interactively" with the computer system as a graphics display is being shown. The operator can, for example, vary certain parameters that pertain to the display being shown and can immediately see the results of these variations on the CRT screen or other display device. Perhaps an engineer is designing a new airplane and has a picture of the shell of the aircraft displayed on a CRT screen. If the shape of the tail of the plane is altered in a certain way, will severe air turbulence result? Interactive communications between the engineer and the computer can give the engineer the answer to this question. Or, perhaps a company vice president is displaying a graph of projected company profits for the next five years on a CRT display station. If he increases financial outlays for advertising at the rate of 10% for each of the next three years, and discontinues operations of an unprofitable division next year, how might the five-year profit picture apper? Again, interactive communications with the computer can result in an immediate response, producing a new five-year pictorial projection on the CRT.

Computer graphics is also used to display dress patterns, design car bodies, show highway layouts and the piping layout on ships, study molecular structures, aid in the design of ships and buildings, display functional mathematical graphs and flowcharts, aid in designing electrical circuitry, display contour maps and weather maps, predict antenna radiation patterns, plot a course for ships and aircraft, display stock performances and show the projected path of hurricanes.

Computer graphics display

COMPUTER AIDED INSTRUCTION (CAI) is a relatively new term and refers to the use of computers for teaching purposes. Its use has grown tremendously. CAI is used in elementary schools, secondary schools and colleges. In some areas, it is even used for pre-school children. CAI is used to teach mathematics, reading, writing, computer programming, history, psychology and almost every other subject.

CAI has many advantages. It is interesting and entertaining. It can relieve teachers from many of their routine and repetitive duties. It provides individualized instruction. It can speed the teaching process. It provides an immediate "correct" or "incorrect" response to a student's answer. It can project student's learning difficulties, and CAI can keep accurate records and summarize data.

Basically, CAI works by providing a tutorial dialogue between the student and the computer. Most commonly, the student is instructed from a CRT computer terminal that has an attached keyboard. The computer talks to the student by displaying messages on the CRT, and the student talks to the computer by typing his or her messages into the keyboard. An example of a third grade lesson might appear as follows . . .

Computer: Good morning Billy. Are you ready for today's math lesson?

Student: Yes.

Computer: Good. Let's begin with some multiplication problems. You seem to be doing very well with this type of problem. How much is 4 times 10?

Student: 40

Computer: Correct. How about 8 times 10?

Student: 80

Computer: Very good. Now let's try some more difficult problems. How much is 6 times 14?

The same tutorial type of instruction can be used regardless of the student's age or the subject matter. Medical students use CAI to arrive at treatments for various computer supplied diagnoses. Ninth grade students are taught the BASIC computer programming language by use of CAI. A bed-ridden sixth grader responds to a computer's math questions over the telephone by keying in his answer on the touchtone pad. And, in Minneapolis, a Holland Elementary School student studies the circulatory system of a fish by viewing the color picture on his CRT terminal.

COMPUTER USAGE IN MEDICINE has grown by leaps and bounds in recent years. One of the more obvious uses of computers in this field is that of record keeping. Hospitals, for example, generate a tremendous amount of data for each patient. Records are needed to keep track of the patient's name, address, phone number, attending physician, room number, diagnosis, treatment, drugs administered, number of days stay and charges incurred. Bills and insurance forms must be printed and payments must be recorded. Statistics are accumulated and reports are prepared.

But the use of computers in the field of medicine goes far beyond that of a record keeping function. Computers are used to monitor many of a patient's bodily functions such as heartbeat, respiration rate, body temperature, brainwaves, blood oxygen, blood flow, galvanic skin response, urine output and chest drainage. They are used to monitor the fetus during labor and the body's vital signs during the administration of anesthesia.

Computers control laboratory testing of urine samples and blood. They can collect and assimilate all data on a patient and notify the physician immediately of any urgent medical situation. They help doctors make medical diagnoses. A computer can analyze an EKG in only minutes after asking itself 5,000 questions. They can measure eye movements for the purpose of detecting balance disorders, and can help the blind to read by converting written text into a spoken language.

WORD PROCESSING is a phrase used to describe another relatively new, but rapidly expanding area of data processing. Word processing refers to a new method of text entry, editing and output.

Most word processing systems consist of a CRT terminal with an attached typewriter-like keyboard. A typist enters information into the keyboard. As the information is keyed, it is displayed on the CRT and simultaneously stored in a memory within the word processing system. Nothing is actually typed until the operator pushes a button and commands the system to print the text.

IBM's Displaywriter, used widely in word processing applications

So what's the big deal? Why bother going through all that? Why not just type it on a typewriter initially? Actually, there's a lot that can be done with the text once it is keyed into the word processing system. For example, at any point the operator can stop typing and go back to any previously typed portion of the text. Any word or string of words, or an entire paragraph can be inserted, changed or deleted. There's no correcting fluid to use. This also means the typist will never have to re-type an entire page because one word was accidentally omitted.

Since the text is stored in a computer memory, it can be recalled as often as the operator wishes. Just push a button, and as many original copies of the same letter can be printed as desired. The text is automatically set in the proper format as it is keyed in.The operator never has to worry about where one line of text stops and the next begins, or where one page stops and the next begins. There is less operator fatigue. Some sophisticated systems are able to catch spelling mistakes and point them out to the operator. The most sophisticated can actually correct any spelling errors for the operator!

But the real payoff in word processing systems is greatest in certain industries and professions which use repetitively typed information. A perfect example is the legal profession. By using word processing, a lawyer's office can produce many original copies of the same legal document, altering only the name or names of the parties involved. Imagine how much time can be saved on the many similarly-worded legal contracts that pass through a lawyer's office daily. Another good example is a company that sends out large volumes of form letters, usually for advertising purposes, altering only the name and address of the individual or company to which the letter is addressed. Here again, the operator need type only the name and address for each letter, the computer does the rest.

COMPUTER CONTROL is a broad based term used to describe a computer system that controls some process. Frequently that process is a mechanical one. A robot is one of the better known uses of computer control. And there are many computer control systems in use today. We encounter them frequently without realizing they exist. For example, many of today's automobile manufacturers use microcomputer (very small computer) control systems. They are used to monitor and adjust the fuel mixture automatically according to altitude, barometric pressure and temperature. They are used to display the car's speed by use of a digital speedometer, or warn of mechanical and electrical problems with diagnostic warning lights. They are used to control the ignition system, regulate the number of cylinders in use, and even unlock the doors by the use of coded buttons.

Computer control systems are used to control the heating and air conditioning systems in buildings. Without this control, the rays of the sun force the temperature control systems of many large buildings to simultaneously run the air conditioning system on one side of the building and the heating system on the other side! Computer control systems are used to control the shape of manufactured objects by a process known as Numerical Control Programming, and they are used to speed production lines and relieve people from tedious and dangerous tasks.

LAW ENFORCEMENT has received a tremendous boost from the field of data processing. Criminal records, once requiring thousands of square feet of building space for storage and dozens of file clerks for maintenance, can now be stored and accessed electronically. Millions of pieces of information on names, dates, license plate numbers and descriptions can be accumulated, stored and accessed in a fraction of the time that was required to do the same tasks by hand.

In El Paso, Texas, for example, the police department's records and identification division has computerized their entire record keeping operation. The installation of a new computer system has replaced a hand system which involved ten tons of manually maintained records in 140,000 individual manila envelopes. The new system has the capacity to maintain 750,000 documents in an area one quarter of the size originally required.

Computers can also aid in police communications. Some police communications departments are so busy it is frequently impossible for an officer in his patrol car to contact the dispatcher at police headquarters. The Palm Beach, Florida, Sheriff's Department had this problem until mini-computers were installed in their patrol cars. By keying license plate numbers into a telephone-like keyboard on the mini-computer, a cruising patrolman can bypass the dispatcher and directly access the computer at headquarters. In less than eight seconds the patrolman will know whether the license number he keyed in is that of a stolen vehicle, who the registered owner is, and if the owner is wanted by the police.

One of the most fascinating stories of computer-aided law enforcement comes from Los Angeles, California. The Los Angeles Police Department is using a computerized crime detection system called PATRIC, which stands for "Pattern Recognition and Information Correlations." They have the ability to supply their computer system with detailed information about a crime for which they have no suspect. PATRIC responds by analyzing this information and supplies the department with a list of names of possible suspects! It does this by cross-checking its data banks for information on previous crimes that have been committed in a similar way.

LIBRARY SCIENCE is taking on a new look as the bound book is replaced by the computer terminal in some applications. And the library is the perfect place for a computer! There are millions of pages of information in tens of thousands of books, and each book has its own number. Computers excel in situations of this kind.

In De Kalb, Illinois, the Library Computer System uses a sophisticated computer network of 275 terminals to link together eight million volumes in 17 libraries across the state of Illinois. A user can browse through the stacks electronically and request a particular book by typing in the book's title and author's name. If the book is available, it will be delivered within three days.

Computerized library systems are becoming popular around the country in both public and private libraries. In Dublin, Ohio, the Online Computer Library Center, Inc., serves 2,400 libraries across the country, and the Southern Library Network, Inc., serves 260 libraries in states from Louisiana to Virginia.

ARTIFICIAL INTELLIGENCE is a term used to describe the "intelligence" of a machine, or more specifically, a term used to describe a "thinking" machine.

We all know that, to an extent, we have intelligent machines. If the temperature becomes too hot in a blast furnace, a computer can reduce the amount of oxygen fed to the flame. If a missile starts to go off course, a computer can correct its path. But such actions cannot truly be described as a thought process. The computers were programmed in a predetermined fashion. They didn't really think about what they were doing.

But is it possible for a machine to really think?

"Computers can calculate, not think," some claim. A computer doesn't learn from its mistakes and a computer cannot originate thought, although careful programming can help computers mimic these human abilities. Computers cannot think . . . today, that is. But will they in the future? What is your opinion?

8

Thorns Among The Roses

You have been looking at the data processing field as a potential career, as something you want to do. The process of finding a position in this field has been presented in an optimistic light because so many people have been successful in the industry, and have enjoyed being a part of it. In fact, this *is* a good time to get involved.

But there are potential thorns among the roses. The benefits of job security, prestige, and high pay don't come to data processors automatically. Instead, the industry requires an investment of time, energy, and personal interest. It is an exacting field for the most part, and when dealing with computers, you'll rarely find a time when "almost right" will do. If something isn't perfect, it probably won't work. Period.

In general, data processing is a "pressure" type job. Whether you are a Data Entry Operator at the low end of the totem pole or the Data Processing Manager at the top end, you'll find pressure at some point in your career, and perhaps frequently.

For example, a Data Entry Operator will find the job requires much attention to detail. Frequently, hours will be spent on the same source document, or on the same type of material. The position might require entering the same information from the same type of documents for days on end. This means, of course, that there is the potential for boredom.

"ZZZ - ZZZZZZZ . . ."

A Data Entry Operator will also find that accuracy counts. To this end, there may be an error-rate which has to be bettered. There may also be hourly, daily, or weekly quotas for the number of documents entered. Add to this the likelihood that not all source documents will be as legible as they should be.

Jobs in the data entry area are improving, however, as more and more computer installations change over to the use of CRT screens instead of keypunched cards. This allows an immediate check and the opportunity to correct errors quite rapidly rather than repunching an entire card for a single mis-stroke.

CRT entry devices tend to speed-up the data entry operation overall, which allows operators a little more flexibility. Electronic keyboards are also much easier on the muscles than the older mechanical keyboards, thus reducing fatigue. Even with these improvements, a Data Entry Operator earns his or her pay, which is usually much higher than entry level clerical positions.

The Computer Operator can have one of the more interesting jobs in the department. This is because the operator often becomes involved with almost every facet of the organization, as so many functions have become computerized.

However, boredom can be a factor for a Computer Operator, especially in larger operations where a single job may well run for several hours. During these periods the operator may simply change paper several times, or change tape reels once or twice. Also, in larger operations there may be specific computers on which only accounting programs are run, for example.

The Computer Operator may also suffer whenever someone else makes a mistake. If a program "dumps" or fails to run for some reason, a programmer may blame the operator. Likewise, the systems analyst or even the Data Processing Manager may make the Computer Operator a scapegoat at times, though this happens infrequently in a well-run installation.

A problem facing all data processing personnel is the "high profile" of the position. We've all been entertained by the various media accounts of computer disasters, which always seem funny when they happen to someone else. For example, a few years ago the shareholders of a large, New York-based company received a quarterly report that included a paragraph that read something like this: "Profits for the quarter dropped fifty percent in comparison with last quarter. There are several reasons for this earnings decline. Market conditions have been poor in recent months, and overseas operations in particular have suffered. In addition, we have experienced difficulties with that portion of our accounting system that was computerized last year. Processing errors resulted in the loss of our entire accounts receivable file, amounting to fifty million dollars. We have recovered forty million dollars of that amount but have been forced to write-off the remaining uncollected receivables. This has resulted in a pre-tax loss of ten millon dollars for the quarter."

Fifty million dollars! That's a lot of money! Here, no doubt, the entire computer and data processing staff suffered from the high visibility and accountability of their positions. We don't know the exact cause of the error. It might have been an error made by a Data Entry Operator. It could well have been a mistake by a Computer Operator. It might also have been an error made by a Programmer or by a Data Processing Manager.

The problem above seems to prove the saying found among some computer workers:

To Err is Human
To Really Foul Things up
Requires a Computer

One northeastern state recently mailed a strange form to many of its residents. The form was called "APPLICATION FOR LICENSE RENEWAL FOR THOSE WHO FAILED TO RECEIVE RENEWAL FORM." The accompanying letter informed drivers that there was a "processing error" that resulted in the loss of a large portion of their records. Because their records are computerized, it is apparent that a computer processing error of some kind was responsible.

Here, too, we can't be sure where the error occurred. Nevertheless, in many data processing applications a single mistake can be extremely costly.

This brings us to the major problem frequently faced by all data processing personnel: time. Computer industry staffers will find themselves on call occasionally, and in some organizations they will be on call constantly.

Many of the people in the computer field actually enjoy this kind of a schedule. Others are willing to endure it because of the job benefits.

Most people outside of the computer field do not understand the lead-time involved in computer work; in fact, they do not understand very much about computers at all. They have deadlines and schedules which must be met and the data processing staff is also forced to meet those deadlines.

This is especially true in operations like payroll check printing where your fellow employees are counting on you as much as the boss is.

Another side of this ignorance is reported by private programming services. These services are frequently small operations – perhaps only a single freelance programmer. When dealing with normally rational, intelligent people, these freelancers may find themselves faced with irate and unthinking reactions when their customers suddenly realize that computers are not necessarily the answers to *all* of their business problems.

In one case, a computer service reports that a doctor whose financial operations had been computerized began demanding a listing of which patients had which diseases, and what treatments had been used on those patients. While computers may well be able to do everything the doctor was demanding, his own system was designed as an accounting system. The information he was requesting had never been entered into the system and had it been, it would have been useless without a program designed to compile and collate those facts in the fashion he requested.

On another occasion a businessman with a small computer system began having unexpectedly rapid success. His computer had handled his initial sales volume with no problem, but with a new sales line and exponentially increasing orders, it was overwhelmed. His irate response? He demanded that the small system be reprogrammed instantly to handle tasks and volume far beyond the design capability of the hardware.

In this case, "instant reprogramming" was impossible. A new program requires thought and study, especially one meant to handle projected changes.

The unrealistic or unreasonable expectations of management may cause many difficulties for data processing personnel. At times, good workers will leave jobs out of frustration, or be fired, because management fails to understand the capabilities of the equipment. In some cases, the salesman might have oversold the system, or the data processor might have oversold his or her ability. Most frequently, however, the management team has failed to do the proper homework, and it is the computer specialist who suffers.

Finally, the sheer seductiveness of computer work can itself be a problem, especially for analysts and programmers. Programming is almost addictive to some people. Many would rather sit at a computer terminal or at their desk working on a program well into the night than go home for dinner. The joy of problem solving that some programmers have leads them to work every available waking hour. And, sometimes, a management will encourage its salaried people to work long hours.

It does happen. Long-time programmers can tell you of acquaintances who worked a week with five hours sleep to finish a project, and then turned around two weeks later to do the same thing again! In passing, the programmer might then mention that the acquaintance became divorced or separated in the midst of the project and didn't even seem to notice.

In short, the data processor, involved in a constantly changing and challenging environment, should enter the field with eyes open. It *is* possible to get a good job in data processing, to keep the good job, and to also have a good life. Knowing some of the potential problems may help you keep your perspective when times get rough, as they may in any job.

Data processing is a good field in which to work, and for some people it is the *ideal* occupation. Hopefully, this book will get you started on your road to success!

9
Key Information Sources

PERIODICALS

ACM Communications
Association for Computing Machinery
1133 Avenue of the Americas
New York, NY 10036

Published monthly by the Association for Computing Machinery. Covers broad scope in the field of information processing. Typical articles include research and development in the areas of computer graphics, computer aided education, computational linguistics and business and scientific computing systems.

Byte
P.O. Box 590
Martinsville, NJ 08836

Published monthly. This is a very large magazine (about 400 pages per issue), which describes itself as the "Small

Systems Journal." Articles are aimed at both the personal computer enthusiast and the small systems users. This publication currently claims to be the world's most widely circulated computer magazine. Each issue contains many advertisements.

Computers in Biology and Medicine
Pergamon Press, Inc.
Maxwell House
Fairview Park
Elmsford, NY 10523

Published quarterly. Deals with use of computers in medicine and the field of bioscience.

Computers and Chemical Engineering
Pergamon Press, Inc.
Maxwell House
Fairview Park
Elmsford, NY 10523

Published quarterly. Deals with computers in the field of chemical engineering. Intended primarily as a record for new developments in the application of computers to chemical engineering problems.

Computers and Education
Pergamon Press, Inc.
Maxwell House
Fairview Park
Elmsford, NY 10523

Published quarterly. Each issue contains four or five major articles dealing primarily with the teaching of subjects which involve computer technology, such as computers and education or computers and banking. Principal emphasis is placed on undergraduate and graduate usage at college.

Computers and Electrical Engineering
Pergamon Press, Inc.
Maxwell House
Fairview Park
Elmsford, NY 10523

Published quarterly. Deals with computers in the field of electrical engineering. Serves to analyze the relationship between computer technology and electrical engineering.

NOTE: The four periodicals listed above are just a few of the computer related magazines published by the Pergamon Press, Inc. Additional magazines published by this company are listed below. The titles are more or less self-explanatory. Most of these are actually quarterly journals, and some carry rather high price tags. Write the publisher for information and prices on any journals in which you are interested.

Computers and Chemistry
Computers and Fluids
Computers and Geosciences
Computers and Graphics
Computers and Industrial Engineering
Computers and Mathematics With Applications
Computers and Operations Research
Computer and Structures
Computer Languages
Computers, Environment & Urban Systems

Computers and People
Berkeley Enterprises, Inc.
815 Washington Street
Newtonville, MA 02160

Published every two months. This magazine would capture the interest of a wide variety of individuals involved in data processing. It is written in a not-too-technical language. Features include articles on the design and application of computer systems for use in business, education and many other fields.

Computerworld
CW Communications, Inc.
Box 880, 375 Cochituate Road
Framingham, MA 01701

Published weekly. This is a very popular newspaper-like publication which describes itself as "The Newsweekly for the Computer Community." Articles cover a broad area including news on recent products, uses of computers in various fields, financial information on companies in the computer field and technical articles for computer users. This is an excellent periodical.

Computer Magazine
IEEE Computer Society
Suite 201
1109 Spring Street
Silver Spring, MD 20901

Published monthly by the Institute of Electrical and Electronics Engineers Computer Society (IEEE Computer Society). Each issue contains about a half dozen major articles. Included are abstracts of technical papers, and articles of general interest on computer systems and computer system design. Other features include conference and workshop reports, and new product reviews.

Computer Decisions
Hayden Publishing Company
50 Essex Street
Rochelle Park, NJ 07662

Published monthly. Covers computers in business, industry and the professions. Written in an easy-to-understand language and geared toward the individual who uses and/or manages a computer installation. Many articles deal with practical solutions to common problems involved with the usage of a computer.

Computer Design
11 Goldsmith Street
Littleton, MA 01460
Published monthly. Articles are oriented toward the design and application of digital equipment control systems. Much of magazine is devoted to new product reviews and application briefs. Geared towards electronics engineers but can be understood by those knowledgeable in computer systems.

Computer Music Journal
The MIT Press
28 Carleton Street
Cambridge, MA 02142
Published quarterly. Deals with hardware and software related to music synthesis and analysis by computer.

Computer Times
P.O. Box 13918
Philadelphia, PA 19101
Published monthly. This is a newspaper style magazine of 30 to 40 pages per issue. Covers news of various data processing markets and vendors.

Creative Computing
P.O. Box 789-M
Morristown, NJ 07960
Published monthly. This is an excellent magazine which

covers both personal computing and small business systems. Articles include product reviews, features on various uses of computers, articles on software and hardware and articles on the lighter side of computing, etc.

Datamation
Technical Publishing Company
875 Third Avenue
New York, NY 10022

Published monthly. This is a widely circulated magazine and is very popular among those actively engaged in data processing. Although many articles are technical in nature, the scope of the magazine is broad enough for those who are not technically oriented.

Dr. Dobb's Journal of Computer Calisthenics & Orthodontia
P.O. Box E
Menlo Park, CA 94025

Published monthly. This magazine is published "for users of small computer systems." It runs about eight or ten feature articles every month, many on software. Program listings are often included.

Information Systems News
333 E. Shore Road
Manhasset, NY 11030

Published twice per month. This is a newspaper style publication for those actively engaged in the field which covers recent events and product news.

Infosystems
Hitchcock Publishing Company
Hitchcock Building
Wheaton, IL 60187

Published monthly. A widely circulated magazine which describes itself as "The Information Systems Magazine for Management." Designed primarily for use as a trade journal for those actively engaged in data processing. Articles cover trends in the industry, new product reviews, etc.

Interface Age
P.O. Box 1234
Cerritos, CA 90701

Published monthly. This magazine describes itself as covering "Computing for Business and Home Applications." Indeed it does cover both areas quite well, with articles of interest on different uses for computers.

Journal of the Association for Computing Machinery
Association for Computing Machinery
1133 Avenue of the Americas
New York, NY 10036

Published monthly by the Association for Computing Machinery. This is a high quality, technical magazine published by one of the leading computer societies. It includes research and technical papers on information processing, many on the mathematical theory of computing.

Microcomputing
P.O. Box 997
Farmingdale, NY 11737

Published monthly. A personal computing magazine with occasional articles pertaining to the business world. Contains many featured articles on both hardware and software for the computer enthusiast.

Mini-Micro Systems
221 Columbus Avenue
Boston, MA 02116

Published monthly. An unusual publication in that it is devoted to mini and microcomputer systems for the business world. Most other magazines of this type are concerned primarily with personal computing.

On Computing
BYTE Publications, Inc.
70 Main Street
Peterborough, NH 03458

Published quarterly. This publication is a "guide to personal computing." It features about a dozen articles each quarter on the use of personal computers. It also contains departments on book reviews, game reviews, new products and coming events.

Small Business Computers
33 Watchung Plaza
Montclair, NJ 07042

Published every two months. Contains articles of interest to those involved with small business systems. Eight to ten major articles are included, along with new product reviews, etc.

Softside
P.O. Box 68
Milford, NH 03055

Published monthly. This is a magazine devoted to software and programming in the BASIC language. Each issue contains a number of programs written in BASIC and various articles pertaining to personal computing systems.

Software News
5 Kane Industrial Drive
Hudson, MA 01749

Published monthly. Concerned with latest developments in software products.

REFERENCE MANUALS AND HANDBOOKS

This is a list of some of the most popular and more recent reference manuals and handbooks.

Automatic Data Processing Handbook
Edited by: The Diebold Group, Inc.
McGraw-Hill Book Company
New York, NY

This is a large volume which is broken down into eight sections: Basic Concepts, The Underlying Technology, Computer Systems Design and Installation, Functional Applications of Automatic Data Processing, Managing the ADP Operation, Outside Services for Data Processing, Special Industry Applications of Automatic Data Processing and The Computer Society. The book is comprised of a series of articles on the eight areas above. It is primarily aimed at management and educators in the fields of data processing and business systems, and is not as useful to the beginner as some of the other handbooks.

Computer Dictionary and Handbook
By Charles J. Sippl and Charles P. Sippl
Howard W. Sams and Company
4300 West 62nd Street
Indianapolis, IN 46206

This is a superb handbook which is equally suitable for those who are new to the computer field and for those who have been in the field for years. About two-thirds of this manual is a dictionary of data processing terms. The remaining pages are devoted to a series of articles covering computer systems, personnel, management science topics, operations research and other subjects. There are additional sections for mathematical definitions, statistical definitions, number systems, symbols used in the computer science field, various programming languages and a section on acronyms and abbreviations. This manual is referred to several times throughout this book.

Encyclopedia of Computer Science
Edited by Anthony Ralston and Chester L. Meek
Petrocelli/Charter Publishers, Inc.
641 Lexington Avenue
New York, NY 10022

This is a huge book of over 1,500 pages. It is a compendium of articles on computers and data processing which covers literally every aspect of the field including business systems, scientific systems, hardware, software, the mathematics of computer science, administration, theory and applications. It is truly an encyclopedia, not just a dictionary. It has a stiff price tag but is well worth it. Included also is an appendix of abbreviations, acronyms, mathematical notations, units of measure and numerical tables.

Illustrated Dictionary of Microcomputer Terminology
By Michael Hordeski
TAB Books
Blue Ridge Summit, PA 17214

This is an excellent dictionary for those involved with minicomputers or microcomputers.

Introduction to Computers and Data Processing
Anaheim Publishing Company
1120 E. Ash
Fullerton, CA 92631

This is actually a textbook, but has been included here because it serves as an excellent introductory text for the newcomer—it assumes no prior knowledge of data processing. In addition, it is beautifully illustrated with hundreds of color pictures and drawings to aid the student. Contents include an introduction to the computer, detailed explanations of how a computer system operates, sections on systems analysis, program design, flowcharting, programming languages, programming in BASIC and much more. All material is very well presented by an initial overview of the subject followed by a detailed examination of the subject area. Also available is a student workbook and study guide which is designed to interact with this text.

Learn to Type*
By Robert G. Flanders
Liberty Publishing Company, Inc.
50 Scott Adam Road
Cockeysville, MD 21030

With this patented system, an individual can learn the fundamentals of touch typing in less than 10 hours. This book is highly recommended for beginners or as a brush-up course for experienced typists.

You're Hired!
By A. C. van Roden and Dr. Thomas D. Bachhuber
Liberty Publishing Company, Inc.
50 Scott Adam Road
Cockeysville, MD 21030

Job-seekers and career changers will find this inexpensive 80-page handbook packed with useful information. Included are tips on finding the right job, writing a resume and a cover letter, successful interviews and more.

SOURCES OF ADDITIONAL INFORMATION

The following are sources of additional information on a career in data processing. Many of the items listed are free of charge, others are not. Write the publisher for latest price information.

American Federation of Information Processing Societies
1815 North Lynn Street, Suite 800
Arlington, VA 22209
Booklet—"A Look Into Computer Careers"

Data Processing Management Association
505 Busse Highway
Park Ridge, IL 60068
Booklet—"The ABC's of DP"
Booklet—"Your Career in Data Processing"

National Business Education Association
1906 Association Drive
Reston, VA 22091
Booklet—"Careers in Business"

IBM Corporation
Data Processing Division
1133 Westchester Avenue
White Plains, NY 10604
Booklet—"Introducing Information Processing"
Booklet—"The Computer Age"

U.S. Department of Labor
Bureau of Labor Statistics
Washington, DC 20212
Booklet—"Office Machine and Computer Occupations" (Bulletin no. 2075-6)

Joyce Lain Kennedy
c/o Sun Features, Inc., Box 368
Cardiff, CA 92007
Pamphlet—"Computer Careers—The Complete Pocket Guide to America's Fastest Growing Job Market"

Career Opportunity Index
17371 Mount Wynna Circle
Fountain Valley, CA 92708
Listing of employers of computer scientists.

The Institute for Certification of Computer Professionals
35 E. Wacker Drive
Chicago, IL 60601
Information on how to obtain the "Certificate in Data Processing" and/or the "Certificate in Computer Programming." These are certificates of professionalism in the field of data processing, somewhat similar to the CPA certificate in accounting.

ORGANIZATIONS AND ASSOCIATIONS

American Federation of Information Processing Societies
1815 North Lynn Street, Suite 800
Arlington, VA 22209

The American Federation of Information Processing Societies (AFIPS) is composed of eleven national organizations engaged in the design and/or application of computers and information processing systems. It is dedicated to nonprofit scientific and educational purposes, and acts in behalf of its constituent societies in carrying out programs designed to advance the information processing profession. The eleven constituent societies are as follows:

American Society for Information Science
1010 Sixteenth Street, N.W.
Washington, DC 20036
Dedicated to creation, organization, dissemination and application of knowledge concerning information and its transfer.

American Statistical Association
806 Fifteenth Street, N.W.
Washington, DC 20005
Fosters statistics and their applications.

Association for Computational Linguistics
SRI International
333 Ravenswood Avenue
Menlo Park, CA 94025
Interested in problems involving both languages and computation.

Association for Computing Machinery
1133 Avenue of the Americas
New York, NY 10036
Studies design, development, construction and application of modern machinery, computing techniques and appropriate languages for information processing.

Association for Educational Data Systems
1201 Sixteenth Street, N.W.
Washington, DC 20036
Interested in relationship of modern technology to modern education.

Data Processing Management Association
505 Busse Highway
Park Ridge, IL 60068
Serves the information processing and computer management community. This is a large organization which includes many programmers, analysts and installation managers around the country.

Institute of Electrical and Electronics Engineers Computer Society
Suite 201
1109 Spring Street
Silver Spring, MD 20901

Devoted to theory and practice of computer and information processing technology, and to exchange of technical information among its members.

Instrument Society of America
Box 12277
Research Triangle Park, NC 27709

Interested in theory, design, manufacture and use of instruments and controls in science and technology.

Society for Computer Simulation
P.O. Box 2228
La Jolla, Ca 92038

Promotes advancement of simulation through use of computers and similar devices.

Society for Industrial and Applied Mathematics
117 South 17th Street
Philadelphia, PA 19103

Dedicated to applications of mathematics to problems in industry and science.

Society for Information Display
654 North Sepulveda Boulevard
Los Angeles, CA 90049

Encourages and contributes to scientific advancement of information display.

Here is a list of other organizations and associations:

American Univac Users Association
P.O. Box 462
York, PA 17405
Comprised of companies which have, or are currently contracting for, a UNIVAC computer.

Associated Information Managers
316 Pennsylvania Avenue, S.E., Suite 400
Washington, DC 20003
Members consist of individuals involved with information and records management in offices and libraries.

Association for Computers and The Humanities
Queens College—CUNY
Flushing, NY 11367
Members are interested in computer applications in the fields of music, history, language, arts and related social sciences.

Association for Literary and Linguistic Computing
Literary and Linguistic Computing Center
Sidgwick Site
Cambridge CB3 9DA, England
Comprised of individuals interested in the processing of languages, and linguistic research by computer.

Association for Systems Management
24587 Bagley Road
Cleveland, OH 44138
An international organization of systems analysts and managers.

Association for Women in Computing
407 Hillmoor Drive
Silver Spring, MD 20901
Membership is interested in the organization, education and advancement of women in the field of data processing.

Association for Women in Mathematics
Women's Research Center
828 Washington Street
Wellesley College
Wellesley, MA 02181
This group concerns itself with issues involving women in the fields of mathematics and computers.

Association of Computer Programmers and Analysts
Reston International Center
Suite 808
11800 Sunrise Valley Drive
Reston, VA 22091
Members include computer programmers and analysts. This organization addresses many issues of importance to this group of data processing professionals.

Association of Computer Users
P.O. Box 9003
Boulder, CO 80301
Includes users and prospective users of all types of computers. Evaluates computer products and services.

Association of Minicomputer Users
2 Frederick Street
Framingham, MA 01701
Comprised of anyone using, or interested in, small computer systems.

Association of Rehabilitation Programs in Data Processing
Michigan State Technical Institute & Rehabilitation Center
Alber Drive
Plainwell, MI 49080

This is a nonprofit organization that is devoted to the promotion of data processing as a career for handicapped individuals.

Black Data Processing Associates
P.O. Box 7466
Philadelphia, PA 19103

Interested in the professional development and advancement of minority groups in data processing. Membership is available to anyone, regardless of race or sex.

Common
435 N. Michigan Avenue, Room 1717
Chicago, IL 60611

Organized to provide a medium of exchange for ideas and information for users of IBM equipment, including the IBM System 3, System 32, System 34, System 38, System 7, Series 1, 1130, 1800 and 5100.

Conduit
Box 388
Iowa City, IA 52244

This organization is concerned with instructional computing. It provides a source of computer based instructional material by distributing a wide variety of curriculum units in the fields of chemistry, biology, economics, geography, mathematics and physics, to name just a few. It also distributes information about the use of computers in higher education, and provides aids for authors and developers of computer based instructional material.

Cooperating Users of Burroughs Equipment
c/o Burroughs Corporation, P.O. Box 418
Detroit, MI 48232

Consists of users of Burroughs computer systems.

Data Entry Management Association
16E Weavers Hill
Greenwich, CT 06830

Concerned with the field of data entry. Members include anyone involved with the data entry profession.

Digital Equipment Computer Users Society
One Iron Way
Marlboro, MA 01752

A large organization of users of Digital Equipment Corporation computer systems. Provides for exchange of information on both hardware and software.

EDP Auditors Association
373 S. Schmale Road
Carol Stream, IL 60187

Organized to provide a forum for all those involved with standards and controls in data processing systems.

Guide International
111 E. Wacker Drive
Chicago, IL 60601

Comprised of members who now have, or plan to obtain, a large scale IBM computer system.

Independent Computer Consultants Association
P.O. Box 27412
St. Louis, MO 63141

Provides directory of and lends assistance to free-lance data processors.

Institute for Certification of Computer Professionals
35 E. Wacker Drive
Chicago, IL 60601
Devoted to the development of examinations for data processing professionals which will assure a high degree of competence and professionalism for those taking the exams.

International Word Processing Association
1015 N. York Road
Willow Grove, PA 19090
Organization consists of anyone involved with, or interested in, word processing.

Minicomputer Users Interest Group
Dept. of Computer Science and Statistics
California Polytechnic State University
San Luis Obispo, CA 93407
Users of, or anyone interested in, mini/micro computer systems.

Pascal Users Group
P.O. Box 888524
Atlanta, GA 30338
Comprised of anyone using, or interested in, the PASCAL language.

Society for Computer Applications in Engineering, Planning and Architecture
358 Hungerford Drive
Rockville, MD 20850
Provides a means for exchange of ideas, information and programs for computer applications in engineering, architecture and related fields.

Society of Certified Data Processors
1835 Union Avenue, Suite 325
Memphis, TN 38104

An organization of those individuals who are certified by the Institute for Certification of Computer Professionals.

Society of Data Educators
983 Fairmeadow Road
Memphis, TN 38117

Organized to promote the use and teaching of data processing at all educational levels. Publishes a monthly journal.

Special Interest Group for Computer Personnel Research
c/o Missouri Pacific Railroad
210 N. 13th Street
St. Louis, MO 63103

Interested in the evaluation of, and specific problems involved with, personnel in the data processing field. Members include data processing personnel directors, teachers, managers and psychologists.

Texas Instruments Minicomputer Information Exchange
P.O. Box 2909
M/S 2200
Austin, TX 78769

Users of, or those interested in, Texas Instruments minicomputers.

Use, Inc.
Box 461
Bladensburg, MD 20710

Users of large scale computer systems.

Women in Data Processing
P.O. Box 8117
San Diego, CA 92102

Interested in promoting the advancement of women in data processing. Membership includes men and women at all levels in the field.

Women in Information Processing
1000 Connecticut Avenue, N.W., Suite 9
Washington, DC 20036

Dedicated to the advancement of women in the information processing field. One of its primary purposes is to help women obtain professional contacts through seminars and affiliated groups.

Word Processing Society, Inc.
P.O. Box 92553
Milwaukee, WI 53202

Consists of anyone interested in word processing.

Glossary

This dictionary provides non-technical definitions for some of the more common data processing terms. Particular emphasis is placed on the definition of terms with respect to the way they are commonly used today. Also, this section is an expansion of the terms introduced earlier in this book.

ADP—Automatic Data Processing.
ACCESS TIME—The amount of time it takes a computer to retrieve data which has been requested.
ACRONYM—A word formed from the initial letters of other words. For example, the word FORTRAN is derived from the two words FORmula TRANslator.
ADDRESS—A particular section in CORE storage, denoted by a name or number.
ALGORITHM—A step-by-step process which is used to solve a specific programming problem. An algorithm is usually represented pictorially by a flowchart.
BATCH PROCESSING—A technique of processing data in a computer system, in which the input data is first coded and grouped into batches before being processed.
BASIC—A programming language that can be used for either business or scientific applications. See Chapter 6.
BAUD—A unit of signaling speed in a computer system. One BAUD equals one code element per second.
BENCHMARK—A programming problem which is used to compare the difference in performance between two computer systems.
BINARY—A condition in which there are only two possibilities, such as ON and OFF. The binary numbering system is a system that uses only the numbers 0 and 1.
BINARY CODED DECIMAL SYSTEM (BCD)—A numbering system in which individual numbers are represented by combinations of the numbers 0 and 1. For example, the number one is written as 0001, the number two as 0010, the number four as 0100, and the number five as 0101.
BIT—A single digit in a binary number. Also used to indicate a unit of storage, or information capacity, in a computer system.
BUFFER—A section within a computer that serves as an intermediary data storage area, or isolation area, between two other sections of the computer. The term is frequently used when referring to an intermediary data storage area between an input or output device and the central processing unit (CPU) of the computer.

BUG—An error in a computer program.
BYTE—A unit of computer storage or information capacity.
CAI—Computer Aided Instruction. The use of computers for instructional purposes.
CARD, IBM—A card of standard size, which is usually divided into 80 columns, and is used for the purpose of entering data into a computer system. Coded information is entered into the card in the form of punched holes.
CATHODE RAY TUBE (CRT)—An electron tube, similar to a TV screen, which is used to display information from a computer system.
CENTRAL PROCESSING UNIT (CPU)—The main unit of a computer system. It contains the portion of the system that is used to perform calculations and carry out all instructions contained in a computer program. Also, that portion of a computer system exclusive of all input, output and peripheral devices.
COBOL—A popular programming language used for many business data processing applications. See Chapter 6.
CODE, CODING—A system of symbols. Most frequently used when referring to a computer program. For example: A program is coded.
COM—Computer Output on Microfilm. Instead of printing on paper, some computers can print directly onto microfilm. See MICROFILM.
COMMAND—A word or phrase entered into a computer for the purpose of instructing the computer to perform some function. COMMAND is also used to refer to various programming words that instruct a program to perform a specific function. For example, the command DIV might instruct a program to divide one number by another.
COMPILER—A special program that converts a source program (a program which a programmer has written) into an object program (a program which the machine understands).
COMPUTER GRAPHICS—The process of communicating with a computer pictorially, or by means of pictures and drawings instead of letters and numbers.
CONSOLE—A control unit, usually comprised of a keyboard and sometimes an associated cathode ray tube (CRT), which is used to communicate with a computer for the purpose of transmitting commands and other information.
CORE—The most important area in the central processing unit of a computer. It is a temporary data storage area which is used to carry out all instructions in a program and is used to control the entire computer system.
CORE STORAGE—Same as CORE.
CPU—See CENTRAL PROCESSING UNIT.
CRT—See CATHODE RAY TUBE.
CURSOR—A marker on a cathode ray tube (CRT) which moves up and down and back and forth on the screen. It is usually used to indicate the point on the screen at which data is being entered.
DATA—Basic element of information in a computer system.
DATA ENTRY—Pertaining to the entry of data into a data collection device for the immediate or eventual use by a computer system.
DATA ENTRY OPERATOR—One who enters data into some type of recording device for immediate or future use by a computer system.
DEBUG—To review a computer program for the purpose of detecting and correcting errors.
DISK DRIVE—The mechanical unit used to hold and rotate a magnetic disk storage device.
DISK PACK—A circular, rotating magnetic data storage device and its associated enclosure, or several circular, rotating magnetic data storage devices mounted together as a single unit, and their associated enclosure.
DOWN TIME—The period of time during which a machine, or group of machines, is out of service.
EDP—Electronic Data Processing.
FIELD—Elements of data in a computer storage device which comprise an assigned area for some specific purpose. For example, a name may comprise a field in a computer tape record which occupies positions 1 to 20 in that record. The street address may occupy positions 21 to 40 in the same record, etc.
FILE—A collection of related data records, stored on some type of computer storage medium. For example, a file of names and addresses on a disk storage device.
FLOPPY DISK—A small (approximately 7″ to 14″ in diameter), rotating data storage device which is circular and flat, and somewhat resembles a phonograph record. Floppy disks are usually used as off-line storage devices.
FLOWCHART—A pictorial representation of the flow of a particular process. Most often used to refer to the flow of a computer system or a computer program.
FORTRAN—A popular programming language used for scientific applications. See Chapter 6.
HARDWARE—Machines, and all other physical equipment, used in a data processing system.
HOLLERITH—A widely used system of encoding information into IBM cards.
INFORMATION PROCESSING—A term used to refer to the processing of any and all types of information. Data processing is a somewhat more restrictive term, being a type of information processing.
INPUT—Data which goes into a computer system.
INPUT DEVICE—A device which accepts data into a computer system. A computer keyboard is an input device.
I/O—Input/output.
KEYPUNCH—A machine used to record data into IBM cards or tape by punching holes in the cards or tape.
KEYPUNCH OPERATOR—One who enters data into cards or tape by use of a special device known as a keypunch, which converts data entered by the operator into a series of punched holes in the cards or tape.
LINEAR PROGRAMMING—A specialized mathematical programming technique which is used to find the best solution to a particular problem. It is used for such diverse applications as finding an optimum steel mixture, animal feed mix or blend of gasoline.
LOGO—A slow computer language used by "beginners" to program microcomputers in schools and homes.
LOOP—A self-contained set of computer program instructions which repeats itself a specified number of times.
MACHINE LANGUAGE—A programming language that a computer system understands without translation. All other programming languages must first be interpreted in order to transform them into machine language. Only when a language is translated into machine language, is it actually understood by the computer.
MAGNETIC STORAGE DEVICE—An information storage device which stores data by using the magnetic properties of certain materials. Tape and disk storage are two types of magnetic storage devices.
MEMORY—Any means of storing data electronically.

MICR—Magnetic Ink Character Recognition. MICR is a method of coding data on source documents in which the data is coded with magnetic ink for the purpose of being read into a computer system by a special device known as a MICR reader. This system is used by banks for the purpose of reading information coded on checks.
MICROCOMPUTER—A very small computer system, generally accepted as being from calculator size up to minicomputer size.
MICROFILM—Very small photograph negatives or films of a printed record. By using microfilm, large volumes of printed material can be stored in a small space. The printed material can be read by use of a viewer which enlarges the image.
MINICOMPUTER—A small, general purpose computer system such as you might find in a small business.
OBJECT PROGRAM—The program that is produced when a source program (a program that is written by a programmer) is compiled. An object program is a machine language program.
OCR—Optical Character Recognition. The machine sensing of printed or typed characters by use of photosensitive devices.
OFF-LINE—An operation in which data being entered or data being put out by a computer system is not under direct control of the central processing unit of the computer. A keypunch operator entering data into IBM cards, is an example of an off-line operation.
ON-LINE—An operation in which data being entered into or data being put out from the computer is under direct control of the central processing unit of the computer. A data entry operator keying information into a CRT terminal that is connected to the computer is an example of an on-line operation.
OUTPUT—Data being put out from a computer system.
OUTPUT DEVICE—Device which puts out data from a computer system. The most common output device is a printer.
PERIPHERAL EQUIPMENT—All auxiliary equipment that is not part of the computer itself. Most pieces of peripheral equipment are input/output devices such as card readers and punches, magnetic tape units, etc.
RANDOM ACCESS MEMORY (RAM)—Pertaining to the ability to immediately retrieve information that is needed. For example, a disk is a random access storage device because it is physically possible to immediately get to the name ZULU in a list of names that are arranged alphabetically. A tape is not a random access storage device because to get to the name ZULU, the entire tape must be read sequentially starting with the A's, reading through the B's, through the C's and so on until the name ZULU is found.
READ—To sense information. For example: A computer reads information stored on magnetic tape.
REAL TIME—Pertaining to the immediate execution of a program, producing results which can be used to control a process or event as it occurs.
RECORD—A group of related fields on a computer storage device. Records can be stored in cards, on tape, on disk and on other computer storage devices.
REGISTER—An area of computer storage which is used to store a specific amount of data, usually for a short period of time, during which some calculation or operation is performed on the data.
REMOTE—Pertaining to the operation of equipment at a remote location, such that communications with the computer must be done over phone lines.
RESPONSE TIME—The period of elapsed time between the initiation of an inquiry at a data terminal, and the time that the answer to that inquiry is received.
RPG—Report Program Generator. A programming language used for business applications. See Chapter 6.
SEEK—To look for data. For example, a computer seeks data on a disk storage device.
SERVICE BUREAU—An organization which provides data processing services for customers that have no computer of their own.
SOFTWARE—Programs, and all other items not classified as hardware, that are needed to run a computer system. Generally, this term is used to refer to computer programs.
SORT—To arrange data records in a specific sequence.
SOURCE DOCUMENT—The document, usually a piece of paper, from which information is read by a data entry operator.
STATEMENT—A line of coding in a computer program.
STORAGE—Pertaining to the retention of data in CORE, or the retention of data on a computer storage device such as on tape or disk.
SUBROUTINE—A sub unit of a program (actually a small program in itself) which is contained either within the main program, or external to the main program. A subroutine is executed by being called into the main program with a single statement. EXSR SUBR1 is a command in the RPG II language which tells the main program to call in a subroutine named SUBR1.
SYNTAX—Rules which pertain to the patterns of formation of statements in a programming language.
TABLE—A collection of data which may be referenced by a program. For example, a table of state abbreviations may be stored in a computer. Data which is keyed into IBM cards can then be checked against this table to make sure that proper state abbreviation codes have been used.
TAPE—A long, thin strip of material which is used as an information storage device. Data can be stored on tape in the form of punched holes or magnetic characters.
TAPE DRIVE—The mechanical unit which is used to hold and rotate computer tape reels.
TELEPROCESSING—The transmission of data from one point to another. Usually referred to when speaking of data transmitted over telephone lines.
TERMINAL—An input and/or output device used to transmit data to or from a computer system. This term is most often used today when referring to keyboard or keyboard/CRT devices which are used to communicate with a computer system.
TIME-SHARING—The simultaneous use of a computer system by more than one user.
VERIFY—To substantiate or confirm that a condition is true. Used most commonly when referring to the editing of data on a source document, or the verification of data entered into an input device such as a keypunch.
WRITE—To transfer data to an information storage device or an output device. For example: A computer can write a name and address file onto tape from a name and address file that is read from cards.

Index

A

ALGOL, 90
APL, 91
APT, 91
Acronym, definition of, 16, 146
Algorithm, definition of, 16, 146
Applications of computers:
 business, 96-101;
 computer control, 114;
 computer graphics, 107-109;
 law enforcement, 114-115;
 library science, 115-116;
 medicine, 111-112;
 science and engineering, 102-107;
 teaching, 110-111;
 word processing, 112-113
Artificial intelligence, 116
Associations, See Organizations and associations

B

BASIC 52-53, 71, 82-84, 146
Bug, definition of, 16, 147
Business data processing, 21, 96-101
Business languages, See Languages: business

C

CAI (Computer Aided Instruction), 110-111, 147
CAL, 90
COBOL, 52, 70-75, 147
COGO, 91
COMIT, 91
CPU (Central Processing Unit), 8-11, 147
Cathode Ray Tube (CRT), 9-11, 16, 108-109, 112, 118-119, 147
Central Processing Unit (CPU), 8-11, 98, 147
Channel controller, 9-11
Command, definition of, 16, 147
Communication controller, 10-11
Compile, definition of, 16, 147
Computer applications, 93-116
Computer control, 114
Computer Equipment Operator, 23-25
Computer graphics, 107-109, 147
Computer, how it works, 8-11, 14-15
Computer mainframe, 10-11
Computer Programmer, See Programmer
Computerworld, See Periodicals
Controllers, functions of, 9-11

D

Data, definition of, 16, 147
Data Entry Operator, 21-23, 42, 58, 118-120, 147

Data processing:
history of, 93-94;
terms of, 11, 16-18, 146-148
Data Processing Manager, 35-36, 43, 120
Disk, definition of, 8, 16
Disk controller, 9-11
Disk drive, 10-11, 147

E

ENIAC (Electronic Numerical Integrator and Computer), 93-95
Education, recommended, 48-49 (Also, See On-the-job training; Schools, Self-study)
Employment: projected, 4, 5;
statistics, U.S. Dept of Labor, 4
Experience, need for, 19, 21, 28-31, 35, 39-48

F

FORTRAN, 52, 70-71, 79-81, 147
Field, definition of, 16
File, definition of, 17, 147
Floppy disk, 8;
definition of, 147

G

Glossary, 146-148

H

Hardware, definition of, 147
Honeywell's Page Printing System (PPS), 100

I

IBM Datamaster, 97
IBM 6670 Information Distributor, 99
IBM 3033, 98
IBM 3800 Laser Printer, 101
Information processing, definition of, 17
Input, definition of, 17, 147

J

JOVIAL, 91
JOSS, 91
Job titles, 19-20
Job opportunities, 19-38

K

Keypunch Operator, definition of, 147; (Also, See Data Entry Operator)

L

LOGO, 90, 147
LISP, 90
Languages:
algorithm, 89;
business, 71;
computer, 69-91;
list processing, 89;
machine, 17, 69;
procedural, 17, 89;
process control, 89;
scientific, 71;
simulation, 89;
time-sharing, 89;
(Also, See individual languages listed separately)

M

Machine languages, See Languages: machine
Mainframe, 10-11
Microcomputer, definition of, 148
Minicomputer, definition of, 148

O

Off-line, definition of, 148
On-line, definition of, 148
On-the-job training, 59-60
Output, definition of, 17, 148
Organizations and associations, 137-146

P

PASCAL, 52, 71, 85-88
PL/1, 52, 71, 90
Periodicals, 125-132
Peripheral Equipment Operator, 23-25
Printer, 11
Programmer, 27, 120, 123
Programming languages, See Languages
Publications, 136

Q

QUICKTRAN, 89-90

R

RAM (Random Access Memory), 8-9, 148
ROM (Read Only Memory), 8-9
RPG II, 52, 71, 76-78
Random Access Memory (RAM), 8-9, 148
Read, definition of, 17, 148
Read Only Memory (ROM), 8-9
Record, definition of, 17, 148
Reference manuals and handbooks, 133-135

S

SNOBOL, 90
Salaries, 21, 23, 25, 26, 28, 29, 31, 32, 34, 36, 37, 55, 62
Schools, 61-61
Scientific data processing, 21
Scientific programming, 31
Scientific languages, See Languages: scientific
Self-study, 57-59
Small computer system, terms of, 11
Software, definition of, 17, 148
Sources of information, See Periodicals; Publications; Reference manuals and handbooks
Systems Analyst, 32-34, 43, 123
Systems Programmer, 32

T

Tape, definition of, 18, 148
Tape controller, 10-11
Tape drive, 8-11; definition of, 148
Telecommunications Network Operator, 26
Teleprocessing, definition of, 148
Time-sharing, definition of, 18
Type, how to, *Learn to Type** book, 135
Typing, importance of, 42

U

User's Group, 47

W

Write, definition of, 18, 148
Word processing, 112-113

Acknowledgements

The author and the publisher thank the following organizations for the use of their photographs and for their assistance:

International Business Machines Corporation
Copyrighted photos appearing on pages 12, 13, 97, 98, 99, and 112

McDonnell, Douglas Automation Company, St. Louis, Missouri
Photo on page 53

Computer Resources, Inc.
Photo on page 54

Smithsonian Institution
Photo (no. 53192) on page 95

United States Air Force
Photos on pages 100 and 101

National Aeronautics and Space Administration
Photo on page 104

Digital Engineering, Inc.
Photo on page 109